AF334980

Cover illustration: In the sub-arctic climate of the Leningrad front, Soviet naval infantry often adopted items of Army uniform. This is a Baltic Fleet patrol, November 1942.

Soviet
Army Uniforms
in World War Two

STEVEN J. ZALOGA

ARMS AND ARMOUR PRESS

Published in 1985 by Arms and Armour Press
2-6 Hampstead High Street, London NW3 1QQ.

Distributed in the United States by
Sterling Publishing Co. Inc., 2 Park Avenue,
New York, N.Y. 10016.

British Library Cataloguing in Publication Data:
Zaloga, Steven J.
Soviet army uniforms in World War Two.—
(Uniforms illustrated; no. 9)
1. Union of Soviet Socialist Republics.
Armiia—Uniforms—History
I. Title   II. Series
355.1′4′0947   UC485.S/
ISBN 0-85368-678-5

Editing, design and artwork by Roger Chesneau.
Typesetting by Typesetters (Birmingham) Ltd.
Printed and bound in Italy.
by Tipolitografia G. Canale & C. S.p.A. - Turin
in association with Keats European Ltd.

Introduction

In the Soviet Union, the Second World War is popularly called the Great Patriotic War, and this term refers to the fighting that took place from the German invasion in June 1941 through to the final victory over the German Army in the spring of 1945. Nevertheless, the Soviet Army had been involved in warfare for several years before the German invasion: there had been sporadic fighting in the Far East against Japan since the early 1930s, culminating in the major outbreaks at Lake Khasan in 1938 and at Khalkin Gol in 1939; and in the west, the USSR joined with Germany on 17 September 1939 and invaded Poland. However, the Soviet Army saw little fighting against the Poles, and it was the invasion of Finland later in 1939 that became its first real contest. The fiasco in Finland underlined the severe problems of the Red Army, brought about in no small measure by the Army purges of 1938 which had gutted its leadership. The Red Army also annexed the three Baltic states (Estonia, Latvia and Lithuania) in 1940 and seized Bessarabia from Romania.

In spite of attempts at reform in 1940–41 as a result of the Finnish experience, the Red Army was soundly defeated in 1941, losing several million troops. But the German Army had bitten off more than it could chew, and after four brutal years of fighting the Soviet Union finally emerged victorious. It was a narrow victory, and the country was pushed to the very limits of its human and industrial resources: for example, the Red Army was so pressed for troops that, by the end of the war, nearly one-tenth of its strength was made up of women – the only nation to use a sizeable number of female combat troops. Likewise, it will be noted throughout the following pages that the Red Army, lacking sufficient uniforms, frequently equipped its troops with civilian garb. A number of distinct uniform regulations were passed during the course of the war, but shortages meant that these could not always be observed, and some of the wide variations in dress can be seen in the photographs.

The illustrations in this book come from the wartime Tass and Novosti bureaux in the Sovfoto archives in New York, from the Office of War Information files at the National Archives, and from other Russian and private collections. The author would especially like to thank Vika Edwards of the Sovfoto bureau for her patient help.

Steven Zaloga

◄2
1. (Title spread) A Soviet trench line during the River Don fighting in 1943. In the foreground is a PTRD anti-tank rifle.
2. Soviet troops on chemical exercises in 1936.

3. Until 1936, the Red Army still used the old. French Adrian helmet left over from the 1917–20 Civil War. Here, a cavalry patrol on exercise in the Moscow Military District (MD) stops at a peasant well, September 1936. (Sovfoto)

4. Cadets at one of the Junior Military Academies wearing cloth peaked caps – headdress peculiar to these prewar schools.

5. Troops of the Far Eastern Army examine captured Japanese equipment following the Lake Khasan battle in November 1938. The soldier to the right wears the Model 1936 helmet, while the man in the centre wears the *pilotka* side cap. (Sovfoto)

6. A Soviet and a Mongolian soldier shake hands after the conclusion of the Khalkin Gol battle against the Japanese in 1939. The Soviet soldier on the right wears the Model 1936 helmet.

7. Soviet signal troops on exercise in the Kiev MD in January 1939. These troops are wearing the *shelm* headgear, developed during the Civil War and replaced by a fur cap in 1940. (Sovfoto)

5▲　6▼

7▼

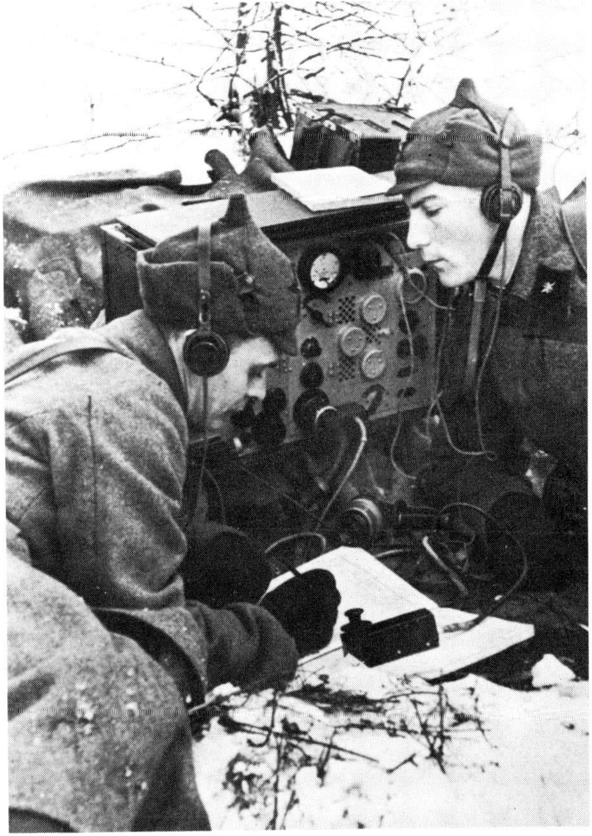

▲8   ▼9

10▲

◄11

8. Soviet troops inspect an inventory of small arms taken from defeated Polish troops in September 1939.
9. Soviet cavalry troops enter Wilno, Poland, September 1939.
10. A horse-drawn Soviet artillery unit enters Poland in 1939. In the background, a BA-10 armoured car tries to pass the mounted troops. The cavalry troops are wearing Model 1936 helmets.
11. A cavalry patrol along the southern Soviet border in June 1940. The troops are wearing the Model 1938 sun hat which was issued for use in the arid regions of southern and south-eastern Asia. (Sovfoto)

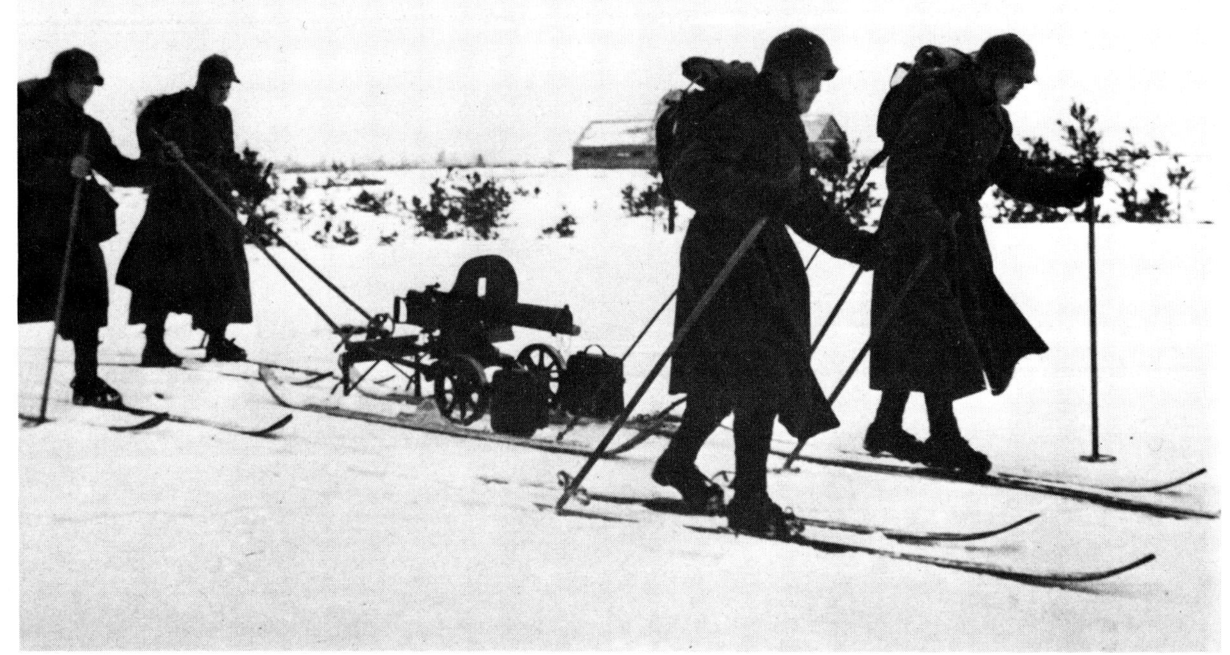

▲12   ▼13

▼14

12. Soviet troops transport a Maxim machine gun on skis. When the Soviet Army entered Finland in November 1940, it was poorly equipped to fight in winter conditions, and paid a heavy price as a result. (Sovfoto)

13. A Soviet ski trooper with a PPSh sub-machine gun. Some Soviet troops were provided with sheepskin coats in February and March 1940 for the final offensive against the Finns.

14. Soviet infantry wearing the Model 1940 fur cap prepare their skis during the February 1941 exercises in Russia. The lessons of Finland were not forgotten, and the Russians would have a distinct advantage over the Germans in the winter of 1941–42. (Sovfoto)

15. Soviet troops during the 1941 fighting. The two soldiers in the foreground wear the Model 1940 helmet, whilst the third soldier still has the older Model 1936 pattern helmet.

16. A machine gunner with the DP 'record player' machine gun supports an infantry attack. He is wearing the Model 1936 helmet which was common at this time.

15▲   16▼

17. The staff of an armoured unit examine a map while their BA-20 armoured car waits in the background. These officers wear the 1940 insignia, and the tanker without the peaked cap is, according to the arm and collar patches, a senior lieutenant.

18. A Soviet motorcyclist scout supports an infantry attack with a 50mm mortar. He is wearing the Model 1940 helmet.

19. A shortage of anti-tank weapons in 1941–42 led to widespread improvisation, especially the use of Molotov cocktails. This photograph also clearly shows the *pilotka* side cap, the most common headgear for Soviet troops during the summer months. (Sovfoto)

20. A Soviet Model 1927 regimental gun in action in the summer of 1941. The old horse-drawn spoked wheel version of this weapon was less common than that fitted with pneumatic tyres.

21. The 45mm Model 1937 anti-tank gun was used by infantry units in the fire-support role; other armies (for example the Wehrmacht) preferred the infantry gun for this purpose.

20▲ 21▼

22. A 45mm Model 1932 anti-tank gun is towed to the front by horse, September 1941.

23. The Soviet Army still made extensive use of cavalry during the Second World War, retaining three cavalry corps and seven independent cavalry divisions in service in 1941. (Sovfoto)

24. Most Soviet heavy artillery was tractor-drawn in 1941. Versions of the Stalinets S-60 tractor (a licensed copy of the US Caterpillar) were common, the example depicted being a ChTZ-65.

25. The staggering losses in troops in the summer of 1941 led to the formation of factory militias like this one from the Kirovski Zavod in Leningrad, famous for its KV tanks.

24▲ 25▼

▲26 ▼27

28 ▲

◀29

26. A cavalry patrol in northern Russia, September 1941. Most Soviet cavalry during the war was raised from Cossack regions in the south after attitudes towards the Cossacks were relaxed owing to the desperate need for troops.

27. An artillery crew of the 25th Chapaevskiy Rifle Division manning a 76mm F-22 field gun in 1942. They still wear the *shelm* winter cap.

28. The need for tanks in 1942 was so great that obsolete types like this T-27 tankette had to serve for the basic automotive training of new crews.

29. With the Baltic Fleet sunk or pinned into its harbours by the Kriegsmarine, a considerable force of sailors was freed to assist in the defence of Leningrad; during the war, Soviet sailors were thus far more likely to see combat on land as naval infantry than on board ship. (Sovfoto)

30. An anti-tank crew wheels out an improvised 45mm Model 38 anti-tank gun from a hidden bunker on the outskirts of Leningrad in the winter of 1941–42.

31. The experiences in Finland in 1940 encouraged the Red Army to pay special attention to ski troops, and these were used with considerable success in the defence of Moscow.

32. A ski troop detachment on patrol. The strange swollen appearance of the headgear of the soldier on the right stems from the fact that the winter camouflage suit hood is being worn over a large fur cap.

33. Flag signalling was still common in the Soviet Army in the early years of the war until the production of radio sets met demand in 1944–45.

34. Soviet infantry support a T-34 Model 1941 tank in the Sevastopol fighting in 1942. The soldier to the left is armed with a bipod-mounted DT tank machine gun, a weapon issued to the infantry in some numbers.

35. An anti-tank position. The soldier in the trench nearest the camera is armed with a Moisin-Nagant rifle fitted with a rifle grenade; in the background is a PTRS anti-tank rifle team.

◀33

34▲   35▼

▲ 36

▲ 37 ▼ 38

36. The most common air defence weapon in 1941–42 was the 4M, a special mounting of four 7.62mm Maxim machine guns. Here, a 4M is manned by Soviet sailors in the defence of Leningrad.

37. A Don Cossack trooper displays dismounted tactics, using his horse as a shield. Owing to their anti-Bolshevik role in 1917–22, Cossack cavalry units were frowned upon by the Red Army, but in 1941 many were reconstituted and allowed to wear traditional Cossack uniforms.

38. A pair of sixty-year-old Kuban Cossack troopers wearing their traditional black and red uniform; the Terek Cossacks wore similar Caucasian dress.

39. In winter conditions,
Soviet infantry squad
weapons like the DP
machine gun were towed
on small sledges which
also carried extra
ammunition.
40. A battery of Soviet
45mm Model 37 anti-
tank guns. In 1942 a new
version, the Model 1942,
was introduced, but by
this time both types were
barely adequate against
contemporary German
tanks.
41. A Soviet nurse tends
a wounded soldier from
a horse-drawn
ambulance.

39▲

40▲   41▼

▲42   ▼43

42. The only motive power for Soviet medium mortars was human; here, an 82mm PM 41 is being brought into combat by its crew. Mortars were one type of weapon in which Soviet designers excelled.

43. A female nurse bandages one soldier while a sailor with a PPSh Model 1942 and a soldier with a PTRD anti-tank rifle blaze away. In 1942–43 Soviet women saw little combat duty except as nurses or in partisan units, but those with sports training (especially marksmen) were beginning to be assigned to sniper units.

44. A Soviet rifle detachment advances. Soviet infantrymen were notoriously ill-disposed towards wearing helmets, feeling that it was unmanly, and unit commanders often had to impose fines or punishment in order to convince troops of the value of such headgear.

45. A Maxim machine gun position during the fighting in the northern Caucasus, summer 1942. The Red Army usually carried bed rolls rather than knapsacks, rucksacks or other specialized equipment.

▲46

46. An interesting comment on the state of Soviet anti-tank weapons in 1942–43. In the foreground is a PTRD 14.5mm anti-tank rifle team, whilst behind it is a 45mm Model 37 anti-tank gun. Neither weapon was wholly effective against modern German armoured vehicles.

▲47   ▼48

47. A 45mm Model 37 anti-tank gun supports a Soviet infantry attack in the Don region, summer 1942. The 45mm gun was a derivative of the German 37mm anti-tank gun, rebored to permit it to fire larger, high-explosive shells. In this fashion, the weapon could be used for anti-tank and fire support in lieu of the two infantry guns and anti-tank guns that equipped comparable German units.

48. A Soviet infantryman passes the burning wreck of a German PzKpfw IV during the fighting in southern Russia in 1943.

49. Another anti-tank rifle was the PTRS, a complicated weapon compared to the more common PTRD and one that featured a clip-fed magazine instead of the bolt-fed system of the latter.

50. Soviet riflemen offer protection to an 82mm mortar battery during fighting in the Don valley in 1943. The riflemen are equipped with a variety of Moisin-Nagant carbines and rifles.

51. The considerable length of the PTRD is evident in this view of a gun team in the fighting outside Kharkov in 1943. The gunner's assistant is armed with the popular PPSh 'burp gun'. Each infantry regiment was usually equipped with 27 PTRDs.

49▲

50▲   51▼

52. The crew of a 107mm 107-PBHM Model 1938 sight their weapon during the 1943 fighting in the northern Caucasus. Heavier weapons like this were occasionally camouflage-painted with bands of mid-brown over the standard dark green.

53. The crew of an 85mm Model 1939 anti-aircraft gun man their weapon along the banks of the River Neva in Leningrad. Although this gun was comparable in performance to the German 88mm, it was seldom used in the improvised anti-tank role, the Russians considering it to be too expensive for this purpose.

54. An infantry artillery crew tow their 76mm Model 27/39 regimental gun from a hidden bunker on the outskirts of Leningrad. The modernized Model 27/39 was the most commonly used version of this infantry support gun, and had, amongst other changes, pneumatic tyres in place of the spoked wheels of the basic Model 27.

55. A Soviet sniper with a Moisin-Nagant Model 91/30 and a PU sniper sight provides cover for an infantry attack. An RGD Model 33 grenade rests near his elbow.

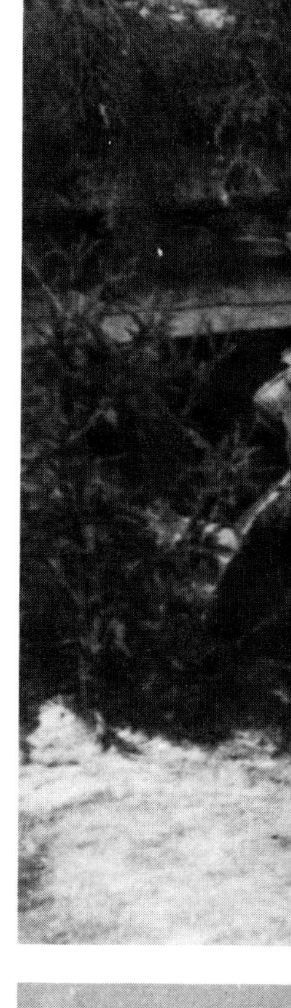

▲52   ▼53

54▲   55▼

56. A fully prepared infantry anti-tank position. The basic weapon is the PTRS anti-tank rifle, but also ready are some RPG-40 anti-tank grenades, a rifle grenade and some Molotov cocktails.

57. Soviet sailors of the Black Sea Fleet played a prominent role in the fighting on the southern front in 1942–43. They retained their naval uniform, although in this photograph several wear the black fur cap developed for naval infantry from the Army Model 1940 fur cap. (Sovfoto)

56▶

▼57

58. The naval infantry of the Northern Fleet were well equipped for the arctic weather, with foul-weather capes for the blustery autumn and spring seasons. The sailor on the left is armed with the relatively rare SVT automatic rifle. (Sovfoto)

59. Soviet infantry in the winter of 1943 wearing the usual winter clothing – Model 1940 fur caps and wool greatcoats. The machine gun crew in the foreground is armed with a DT tank machine gun with a bipod attached. This weapon had a smaller drum magazine that was easier to handle than the ungainly 'record drum' of the DP infantry machine gun, and also a collapsing stock, which made it handier to carry. (Sovfoto).

◀58

59▼

▲60

▲61 ▼62

60. Two of the less common infantry weapons of the Second World War were the SVT40 automatic rifle and the DS Model 1939 light machine gun, both of which are shown here. The cap on the machine gunner is non-standard and is probably a piece of civilian garb put to good use.

61. Soviet infantry embark aboard the Soviet destroyer *Tashkent*. This ship was used for troop landings on the Black Sea coast until July 1942, when it was sunk by air attack at Novorossisk. (Sovfoto)

62. A Terek Cossack unit on patrol in the northern Caucasus in 1942. One of the cavalrymen wears the traditional Caucasian garb, but the others mix this with standard Red Army uniform and riding breeches. (Sovfoto)

63. First invented by the anarchist cavalry leader Makhno in 1918, the *tachanka* became standard equipment in Bolshevik cavalry units to carry the cumbersome Maxim machine gun. These machine gun firing platforms were still in use on the Western Front in June 1942 when this photograph was taken.

64. In a scene reminiscent of the Civil War, a Terek Cossack unit stages a charge for the camera, complete with *shshlik* sabres and *tachankas*. (Sovfoto)

65. A Kuban Cossack cavalry squadron in full traditional dress but with a few modern additions, such as a map case, in evidence. (Sovfoto)

63▲

64▲   65▼

▲66

66. A Bashkirian mounted unit on patrol, May 1943; the distinctive cape of the region is very evident here. The cavalryman on the far right is G. Agadulin, winner of the Order of the Red Star. (Sovfoto)
67. A Soviet infantry squad on the Volkhov Front in April 1943. As the war dragged on, more and more Soviet infantry were equipped with the popular PPSh 'burp gun'. These troops are wearing the *telogreika* padded winter jacket. (Sovfoto)

▼67

68. Soviet infantry in action south of Lake Ilmen, April 1943. The nearest soldier is armed with an SVT40 automatic rifle. (Sovfoto)
69. In the absence of armoured troop carriers, the Russians were obliged to improvise, the most common tactic being to carry troops into combat on tanks (the so-called 'tank desant' troops). These men are moving into action on a KV-1 Model 1942 tank.

70. A patrol of Baltic Fleet sailors armed with an incredible assortment of weapons. At least two have Tokarev automatic rifles like the SVT40, several have a PPSh, one is equipped with a DP machine gun and the nearest figure is armed with a Schmeisser MP40 sub-machine gun captured from the Germans. (Sovfoto)

71. The Black Sea Fleet provided large numbers of troops for the defence of the Kerch peninsula in 1942. These two sailors are armed with Moisin-Nagant rifles. (Sovfoto)

72. Although not trained for the role, sailors were often employed in amphibious landings. The photograph shows a Northern Fleet landing patrol in 1942, armed with SVT40 automatic rifles and PPSh sub-machine guns. (Sovfoto)

73. A 76mm F-22 USV divisional gun in operation in Stalingrad in November 1942. This weapon was a development of the basic F-22 and was succeeded by the ZiS-3 gun in 1942.

▲74

74. An important ancillary force of the Red Army was the Soviet partisans. Here, peasants behind German lines are instructed in the use of Maxim machine guns.

75. During the fighting in the Kursk bulge in the summer of 1943, heavy Soviet defensive lines wore down the German tank attack. This position is armed with both the PTRD and the PTRS anti-tank rifle, which by this time were only effective at very close range owing to the increased thicknesses of German tank armour.

▼75

76▲

76. The standard Soviet heavy field gun of the war was the ML-20 152mm Model 1937; the self-propelled versions were the SU-152 and ISU-152. This battery is in action outside Zytomierz in 1944.

77. A 76mm F-22 USV during the liberation of Kiev. The German Army was very impressed with this lightweight but potent gun, and many examples captured in 1941 were put to good use.

77▼

▲78

▲79   ▼80

78. During Operation 'Bagration' in the summer of 1944, when the German Army Group 'Centre' was destroyed, Byelorussian partisans like these played a crucial role in disrupting German supply lines and tying down troops.

79. A platoon of women snipers of the 2nd Pribaltic Front, commanded by Lt. Nina Lobkovskaya. This unit belonged to a Guards division and, obviously, the women won many decorations for valour in service. Sniping was one important combat role assigned to women in the Red Army; another was driving tanks.

80. Officers of the 143rd Independent Tank Battalion pose before their T-34-85 tank; third from the left is Major V. G. Kulikov, future Marshal of the USSR. Note the use of comfortable and popular civilian sheepskin coats instead of service issue garments.

81. A Soviet partisan cavalry unit marches through a Ukrainian town in 1944. These units were usually incorporated into the regular Red Army once their home territory had been liberated, resulting in some rather motley arrays of uniforms.

82. A Soviet sergeant examines the PPSh of one of his students. Note the popular *pilotka* caps and also the shoulder straps, the latter reintroduced in 1943 having for decades been regarded as the hateful symbol of the Tsarist Army.

81▲   82▼

▲83　▼84

85▲

◄86

83. The role of political commissars shifted as the war progressed from tactical leadership alongside unit commanders to one of a less military character. Commissars became responsible for unit morale and propaganda, and 'sing-alongs' with a unit musician were among the more popular activities.

84. A Soviet tank unit is greeted in the market square of a Ukrainian town in 1944. In the background is a T-70 light tank.

85. A Soviet partisan unit in the Ukraine in 1944. Besides fighting the Germans, these units were also frequently involved in scraps with the nationalist Ukrainian UPA and the Polish AK partisan groups.

86. Soviet troops try to overcome barriers in the defences protecting Finnish positions in Karelia. The Russians knocked Finland out of the war with a massive summer offensive in 1944.

▲87　▼88

87. An anti-aircraft battery armed with the 85mm AA gun is informed that it has been decorated for its performance against the rare German aerial incursions of 1944.

88. Soviet scout troops in action in Finland in 1944. Assault engineers, scouts and snipers were the only troops regularly issued with camouflaged coveralls like these.

89. The PTRD anti-tank rifle was still in service as late as 1944 and 1945. Only marginally effective against tanks, it was nevertheless popular for long-range sniping against entrenched German troops, or against troops in buildings.

90. Soviet troops in winter coveralls advance on the Mozhaisk monastery.

91. The Soviet method of crossing rivers was to seize small bridgeheads with troops using these PK or MPK inflatable rings and hand paddles, and then gradually enlarge the bridgehead. This particular infantry group was photographed during the fighting in the Kuban swamps.

89▲

90▲   91▼

▲92   ▼93

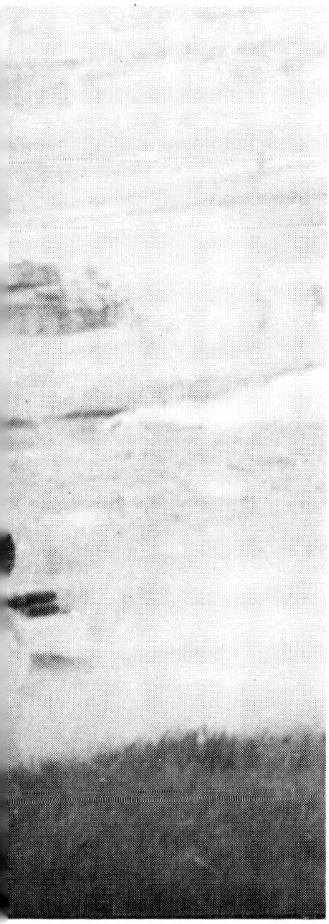

92. A Cossack cavalryman wearing the traditional black fur cap during the Dniepr river crossing.
93. T-34-85 tanks and accompanying infantry advance into Romania with the 1st Ukrainian Front, summer 1944.
94. Another illustration showing infantry using PK rings to ford a river. These troops seem to be fully equipped, and are wearing rubberized wading trousers.
95. An ML-20 152mm field gun in action in the summer of 1944.

94 ▲

95 ▼

96. Troops from a Russian infantry unit chat in a captured Finnish trench on the Karelian isthmus in 1944. Note the Finnish Lahti anti-tank rifle. (Sovfoto)

97. A good view of the padded winter clothing that became common in 1943–44. The preponderance of PPSh sub-machine guns amongst the troops is noteworthy.

98. A scout patrol on the outskirts of a Polish village in 1944.

99. The crew of a 107mm mortar prepare the weapon for firing.
100. When horses fail, use men! Soviet artillery design stressed light weight, for reasons made obvious in this view of an anti-tank unit moving a ZiS-3 76mm divisional gun and a 45mm Model 42 anti-tank gun through a stream in the outskirts of Lvov. (Sovfoto)
101. A Maxim machine gun mounted on a *tachanka* supports a Terek Cossack cavalry charge, May 1944. Cavalry still proved valuable in wooded areas or for scouting.
102. Infantry dig in to repulse German counter-attacks during Operation 'Bagration' on the 1st Byelorussian Front in July 1944.

▲99　▼100

101▲ 102▼

▲103   ▼104

103. A Soviet scout unit enters Augustow, Poland. These scouts wear the distinctive camouflage overalls of elite units. (Sovfoto)

104. A Soviet patrol occupies abandoned German positions in 1944. White camouflage coveralls are still in use despite the change of season.

105. A relative of the ML-20 was the 122mm A-19 Model 31/39 field gun, which featured a longer barrel with no muzzle brake. The Soviet Army often used heavy artillery in street fighting, as a single round could disembowel an entire building. The scene here is Danzig.

106. One of the more ubiquitous types of Soviet artillery was the popular ZiS-3 76mm divisional gun, which could be used either as a field gun or in the anti-tank role. This weapon is being used by the 2nd Ukrainian Front in 1944.

105▲ 106▼

▲107 ▼108

109 ▲

110▲   111▼

107. Soviet troops take Gatchina in the winter of 1944–45, their winter white coveralls having assumed a very dingy appearance!

108. The crews of an assault gun regiment warm themselves by the fire outside Poznan, Poland, in the winter of 1944–45. In the background is one of their SU-152s.

109. The largest foreign units allied to the Red Army on the Eastern Front belonged to the Polish LWP. The troops wore Russian uniforms, with Polish *rogatywka* fatigue caps and Polish insignia.

110. By 1945, Polish troops made up about ten per cent of the Red Army's strength. There were also smaller Czechoslovak forces, as well as Romanian and Bulgarian units once these armies had switched sides. Here, a Polish Maxim crew is shown in action, 1944.

111. A Polish infantry squad advances during the fighting in Poland in 1944.

▲112

112. A Soviet ROKS-2 flamethrower team in action in 1945. The soldier at the right may be fitted with some sort of armoured vest.
113. A Soviet scout patrol in action. These units were often provided with special camouflaged jackets or coveralls.
114. Two Soviet soldiers equipped with ROKS flamethrowers move forward during street fighting in 1945. Flamethrowers were very commonly used in urban combat.
115. A popular morale booster: a sign indicating distances to Berlin and to Moscow.

▼113

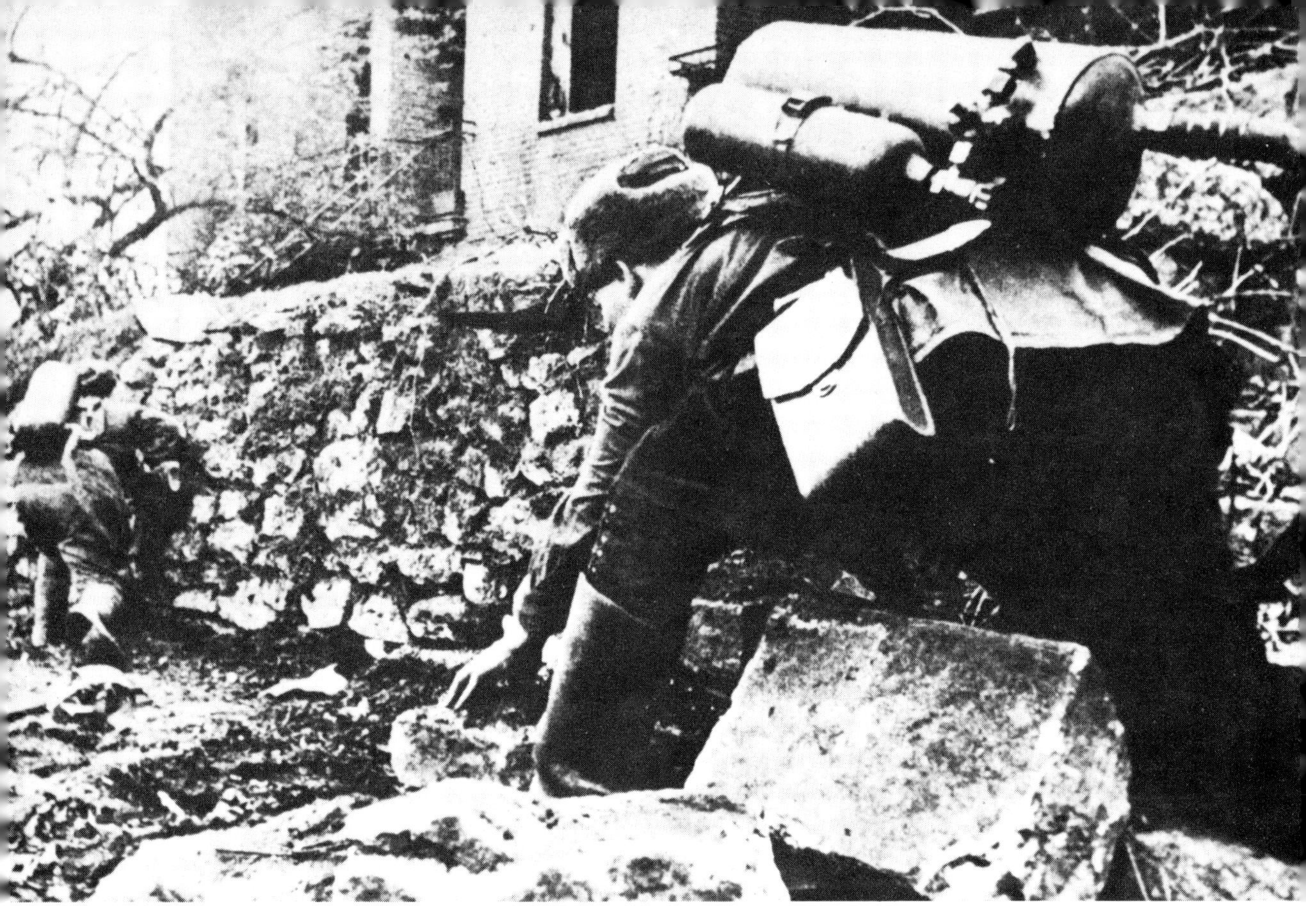

до БЕРЛИНА
129 км.
до МОСКВЫ
1751 км.
ПАВИЛЬОН ОЖИДАНИЯ

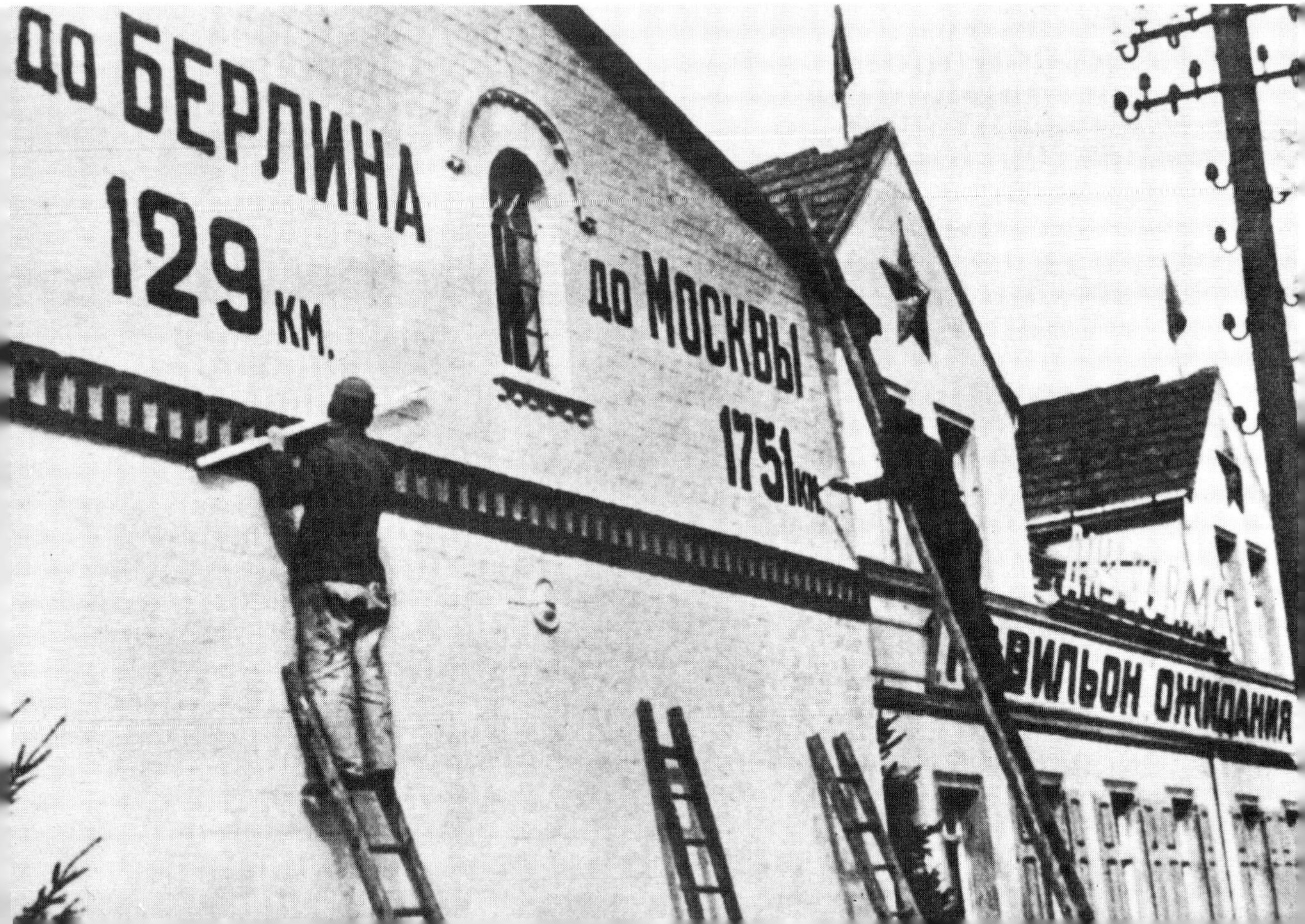

▲116 ▼117

118▲

116. The ZiS-3 was the standard divisional gun of the Red Army during the Second World War, and the equivalent of the British 25pdr and the US 105mm howitzer. It was frequently used as an anti-tank gun.
117. Sr. Sgt. I. I. Gavrish in Wroclaw (Breslau). Gavrish was made a Hero of the Soviet Union, the Red Army's highest military honour for valour, for his performance in Breslau. He is wearing a rain cape, a popular item of equipment and one useful for other purposes, for example as a bed cloth or as a small tent.
118. One of the main advantages of the ZiS-3 divisional gun was that it was small enough to be manhandled. An anti-tank gun, the ZiS-2 57mm, was derived from it.
119. Troops of the 3rd Byelorussian Front pour into Königsberg in January 1945.

119▼

▲120 ▼121

120. Soviet infantry take a breather on the Oder river line in January 1945. By this stage of the war, the fleece-lined fur cap had become the standard winter headgear of the Red Army. (Sovfoto)
121. A Cossack cavalry unit stands-to for inspection in Germany in 1945. The uniform had by now taken on a distinctly standardized form as a supply of traditional clothing for Cossacks could only be found in their homelands. (Sovfoto)

122. Soviet troops enter Gleiwitz, Silesia, in February 1945. Even at this late date, Soviet infantry units were still equipped with the PTRS and PTRD anti-tank rifles. (Sovfoto)
123. Soviet infantrymen enter Schneidemühl, Germany, in February 1945. The winter padded *telogreiki* jackets were often bereft of insignia, which were worn on the uniform beneath. (Sovfoto)

▲124　▼125

124. Soviet infantry manhandle a 76mm Model 27/39 regimental gun in the streets of Gleiwitz, to gain a little extra firepower. Most of these troops are wearing wool greatcoats instead of *telogreiki* jackets. (Sovfoto)

125. One of the major contributions of Lend-Lease to the Soviet 1944–45 offensives was the provision of over half a million vehicles like this Chevrolet 1½-ton truck. Such vehicles provided the Red Army with tactical mobility and adequate supply lines.

126. These scouts were the first Soviet troops to enter Vienna. The mixture of headgear and uniforms was typical of the Soviet Army of the period, especially of units which had been in the field for any length of time. Note the absence of helmets even on combat troops. (Sovfoto)

127. Even as late as 1945, the Cossack cavalry continued to be employed at divisional strength. Here, traditional Kuban Cossack capes are oddly topped by Model 1940 steel helmets. (Sovfoto)

128. The most popular Soviet infantry anti-tank weapons were captured German Panzerfaust rocket launchers and their Soviet copies, RPG-1s, seen here in action in the streets of Berlin.

129. The war concluded, a group of Cossack cavalry officers rests at a German seaside resort. The men are wearing traditional *papachka* astrakhan caps and blue cavalry breeches. (Sovfoto)

▲128　▼129

B–17F's of the 96th Bomb Group, 8th Air Force, heading out for a target in Germany.

THE BOEING B-17 FLYING FORTRESS

The most effective method open to a World War II USAAF instructor anxious to stir a lazy group of students into renewed effort was for him to announce that only the top ten per cent of the class could expect assignment to a B-17 unit; and the eagerness of students to become Fortress aircrew was equalled by the enthusiasm of seasoned veterans. Any one-time Fortress crew member will declare without hesitation that the Boeing B-17 was the greatest bomber ever built.

Many things inspired this confidence in Boeing's bird. Not the least was the abundance of photos showing some shot-up Fort which had limped home safely with its crew aboard. Stories were told and retold about B-17's that came back on three engines, two engines, and in a few instances, on a single engine. Tail surfaces were shot away, huge chunks blasted out of the fuselage, holes blown in the wing big enough to drop the ball turret through, wing tips rolled up, even engines ripped off the wing — none of these disasters seemed to prevent them from finding their way to a friendly base.

The "Queen" was also a beautiful aeroplane, undoubtedly the most graceful of the four-engine bombers, and it had a rugged character to match its photogenic looks.

From a pilot's viewpoint it was a dream plane to fly; it handled easily, held a tight formation without undue strain on the pilot, was stable and forgiving. It also responded to a pilot's touch like a fighter, and these characteristics enabled young crew members who had washed out in primary or basic flying school to take over in an emergency, guide the Fortress back to base and make a safe landing when the pilot and co-pilot were wounded or dead. This happened on a number of occasions.

In the beginning

Boeing designed and built the Monomail, and from the experience gained they proceeded to turn out the B-9, which may be considered as the grandfather of the B-17. Both of these designs were "firsts", and were radically different from other designs of the times. Next in the progression was the Model 247, which pioneered the Boeing transports and gave them a lead that is still unbroken.

From these it was but a step, a giant step at that, to the B-17. Dubbed Project 299 by the company, the prototype had its beginnings on September 26th 1934 when, in a great gamble, $275,000.00 was allocated for the design and construction of Model 299, a four-engine bomber, by the Board of Directors.

Eight months later test pilot Les Tower lifted the 299 off the Boeing Field runway before sunrise on July 28th 1935, for her maiden flight; this first flight was a huge success and delighted all connected with the project. More testing work set the stage for the next important event in the history of the new bomber.

At 3.45 a.m. on August 20th Towers again took off in the 299, but this time he circled the field and pointed her nose East. Nine hours later he brought her down on the runway at Wright Field, after covering the two thousand-plus miles at an average speed of 233 miles per hour. When the Air Corps officers saw the 299 they were awed by its size, and unofficially called it Boeing's aerial battle cruiser; later it was officially designated as the XB-17.

Flight tests were even more impressive, and in the bomber competition with the Martin B-12 and the Douglas B-18, the XB-17 was ahead in all captions.

On October 30th 1935, tragedy struck. The 299 crashed

A Y1B–17A formating with a Pan American Boeing Clipper over Puget Sound, Washington, probably in early 1939. (USAF)

on take-off and burned. Major Pete Hill, the Army Air Corps chief test pilot, died shortly after the crash; Les Tower lingered between life and death, and seemed to be recovering, but suddenly succumbed to his burns and other injuries. Due to the size of the tail-plane Boeing had designed a locking device to prevent the control surfaces from being damaged on the ground by whipping in the wind. Someone had neglected to release these spring locks before take-off, thus causing the crash. The plane was cleared of any mechanical or design failure and although Boeing lost the contract, with their 299 out of the running, the Air Corps had been sufficiently impressed with what they had seen to place an order for thirteen Y1B-17's and a fourteenth airframe for structural testing.

These Y1B-17's were assigned to the Second Bombardment Group for service testing. The Second was based at Langley Field, Virginia, and commanded by Lt. Col. Robert Olds. To his Group went the task of teaching men to fly and fight the B-17's. This in itself was a tall order — but the sceptics and critics of the heavy bomber programme also had to be reckoned with; simultaneously with the training programme, a safety programme was developed. The Group's twelve Forts were flown approximately one and three quarter million miles and logged 9,293 flying hours. This flying was done in all kinds of weather, and not a single aircraft was lost in an accident. The Group, in an effort to publicize the B-17, went after existing records and broke them with ease. They also set records in new categories where none existed previously. A mass goodwill flight to the Argentine was flown in February of 1938 by Col. Olds and his men; the 5,036 mile trip was covered in 26 hours and 50 minutes flying time.

Other records set by Col. Olds included an East-West transcontinental mark of 12 hours and 50 minutes, and a West-East record of 10 hours and 46 minutes. The B-17 was big news in the United States, thanks to the efforts of these men.

Due to what turned out to be a lucky accident the fourteenth Y1B-17 was not static-tested to destruction. A fully loaded and instrumented Fort hit some rough air in a storm over Langley Field. It was thrown into a stall and a spin, but the pilot managed to pull it out and made a safe landing. Although the wings were bent, rivets popped, and the test instruments showed that it had exceeded the G loads for which it was built, it survived the ordeal in repairable condition. Thus it was decided that there was no need to use the fourteenth airframe for the static tests, and instead it was fitted with turbo-superchargers for high altitude flying experiments and retained at Wright Field; it was designated the Y1B-17A. There was only a single example built (S/N 37369) and it differed from the others in that it was fitted with Wright R-1850-21 engines and General Electric superchargers. The fairings over the engine nacelles were also removed.

The B-17B, of which 39 were built, differed from the B-17 and B-17A in that the bombardier's indentation and nose blister were removed, and it was fitted with Wright R-1820-51 engines.

Thirty-eight B-17C's were manufactured, and they featured improved gun emplacements and additional engine improvements. These were followed by forty-two B-17D's which had the more powerful Wright R-1820-65 engine, two additional .50 calibre machine guns, and self-sealing fuel tanks. The D-model was the last of the original design B-17's.

The B-17E made its first flight on September 5th 1941. The aircraft had now been extensively redesigned and it bore only a general resemblance to its predecessors. The rear fuselage and tail were completely new, and two power turrets had been added, along with a twin machine gun "stinger" in the tail. A total of 112 B-17E's were built before it was superseded by the F-model; however, an additional 400 were built with a Sperry ball turret.

The B-17F was mass produced by Boeing, Vega, and Douglas. The big three turned out 3,400 during the production life of the F-model.

The last model in the line was the B-17G, which differed from the F mainly in the addition of the Bendix chin turret which was armed with twin .50 calibre guns, and mounted on the underside of the nose. The G sported a total of twelve .50 calibre machine guns. A total of 8,680 had been built by the time S/N 44-85841 rolled off the line at the end of production.

Combat Operations:

The Far East and South Pacific

It was in this area that the B-17 first made its presence felt by the enemy. When the Japanese attacked Pearl Harbour and the Philippines, it was the B-17 which began carrying the war to the enemy. Once Air Forces were established, the 7th, 19th and 43rd Bombardment Groups (Heavy) were assigned to the 5th Air Force, to form the 5th Bomber Command. The story of these Groups will be treated as a part of the story of the 5th Air Force, although much of their history they made while they operated independently, although they were members of the FEAF.

The 19th Bombardment Group quickly became the most famous bomber unit in the USAAF. Their exploits produced seven Distinguished Unit Citations and a Congressional Medal of Honour among other awards. Many of the pilots and aircraft became legends in their own time. These included *Yankee Doodle Jr.*, *Galloping Gus*, *Madam X*, *Typhoon McGoon*, *Suzy-Q* — and the most famous of all, *Alexander the Swoose*, with the subtitle, *It Flies*.

The *Swoose*, so far as is known, is the only surviving

A pair of B–17D's flying in close formation, the nearest aircraft of the 7th Bomb Group. (USAF)

B-17D in the United States. She is a part of the Smithsonian's National Air Collection but is in storage rather than on display. The *Swoose*, named after a bird that was half swan and half goose, actually started its career as S/N 40-3097; that career was almost brought to a premature close when the Japanese worked her over on the ground at Clark Field. Parts from other Forts in worse shape were removed and used to replace a wing, the rudder and a tail plane, plus a couple of engines. Her first pilot after the major surgery was Lt. Col. Hank Godman, and the *Swoose*, in company with several other " revived " B-17's, did their best to break up enemy convoys and troop concentrations in the Philippines area. The time came when they were forced back to Java and finally to Australia. At Newcastle, NSW, Australia, a new tail assembly and other spare parts were tacked onto the Fort, and it was here that she was given the name of *Alexander, the Swoose*. An insignia of a swoose was painted on her sides and *It Flies* was added, perhaps to prevent some eager beaver from towing her to the scrap pile. Now the *Swoose* began to average 150 hours per month in the air, most of them on combat missions. Finally, as a few newer B-17's arrived, the *Swoose* was eased off combat — but she was not yet ready to become a hanger queen.

Major-General George H. Brett selected her as his personal transport aircraft, and she continued to pile up the hours and miles. Ordered to the Caribbean, General Brett flew from Australia to Washington, D.C., in the *Swoose* and continued to use the plane on his many trips to his new command area. At the war's end she was rescued from the scrap heap by the Mayor of Los Angeles, who proposed to keep her as a war memorial; but in January of 1949 her old crew was gathered together, and flew her to Washington, D.C., to become a part of the National Air Collection. In her career she had flown enough miles to take her around the equator at least 25 times.

Although less well known, the *Suzy-Q* had also compiled an impressive record. It had circumnavigated the globe, a 35,000 mile trip, crossed the equator four times, flown thousands of combat hours, and amassed the highest victory total of any bomber in the theatre. *Yankee Doodle Jr.* sported six Japanese " kill " flags, and was also credited with two ships destroyed. *Madam X* accounted for three Japanese aircraft and a destroyer on her first eight missions.

The 19th Group was the Unit entrusted with the evacuation of General MacArthur, his family, staff, and the President of the Philippines to Australia. There is a story connected with this mission which may be of interest. MacArthur, upon seeing the pilot assigned to his B-17, refused to fly with him because Lt. Harl Pease, Jr., looked too young and inexperienced. Later Pease, then a Captain, won the Congressional Medal of Honour for pressing home an attack in a badly damaged B-17 and losing his life in the process.

The 7th Bomb Group was the unit which was *en route* from California to the Philippines when it arrived over Pearl Harbour in unarmed B-17's, while the Japanese were actually attacking. They managed to land their aircraft in various spots, including a golf course and a Pursuit Field, but all were shot up and damaged in the process. Others in the Group managed to get to their destination because of a difference in time schedules for departures. They fought in the Philippines, then from Java, and finally from Australia as the Allies were pressed back by the Japanese advance. While in Java they were awarded a DUC for their part in holding up the Japanese invasion by bombing convoys, supplies and troop concentrations.

The 43rd Group, after a period of anti-submarine patrols along the New England coast, were ordered overseas and proceeded to the South Pacific via Capetown to join the 5th Air Force. Flying out of bases in Australia they raided enemy targets in the Dutch East Indies and the Bismarck Sea area. The Group practised skip bombing in its spare time, and became proficient at the art. This proficiency stood them in good stead when the Battle of the Bismarck Sea took place, as their part in the action won them a DUC. The 43rd produced not one CMH winner but two, and both were won on the same mission. Lt. Joseph R. Sarnoski, bombardier, and Capt. Jay Zeamer, Jr., pilot, won the nation's highest honour while on a reconnaissance mission. Though under attack by Japanese fighters, and mortally wounded, Sarnoski continued to man his guns and helped fight off the attackers before becoming unconscious. Capt. Zeamer, also badly wounded, still managed with the help of a crew member to bring their B-17 back to base and make a successful landing.

The B-17 was eventually phased out by longer-ranging B-24's and finally by B-29's. While it was in action it compiled a record which was second to none.

North Pacific

Although little has been written about this area the B-17 operated in the Aleutians and Alaska as successfully as it did elsewhere, although conditions and techniques were vastly different. Due to the weather nearly every mission was flown at extremely low altitude. The Forts seldom operated higher than 100 feet above the water, due to the fog that shrouded the target areas. At this altitude bombing results were excellent — it was almost impossible to miss. Many times the target had to be searched out by cruising back and forth until it was spotted. While interception by fighters was no threat, and anti-aircraft fire was negligible, the threat of flying into a " stuffed cloud " was very real. The clouds were stuffed with mountain peaks.

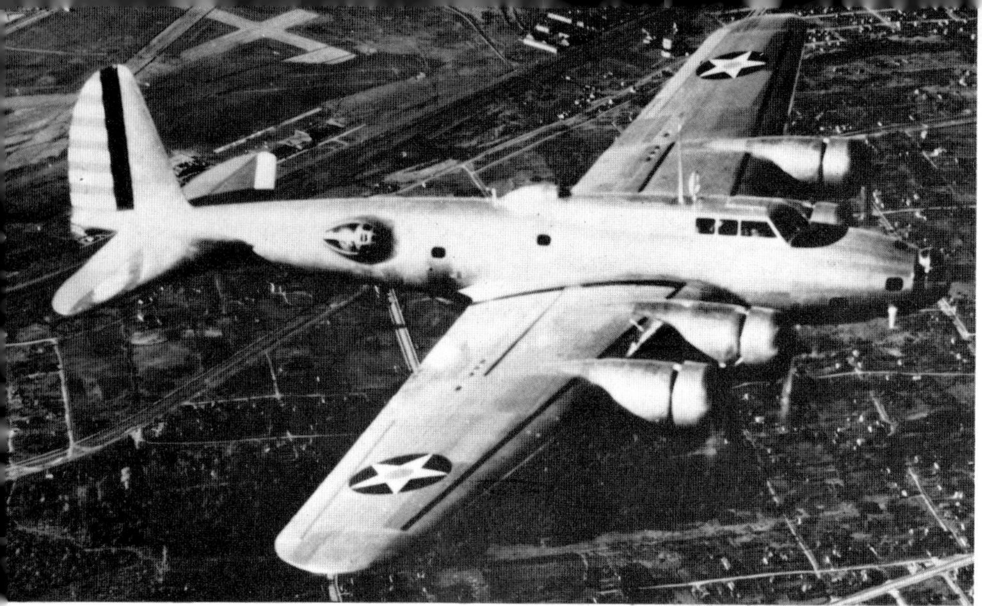

Left: Near plan view showing upper surface details of a B–17, note DF loop ahead of radio mast. (USAF)

Below: B–17D probably from the 19th Bomb Group. (USAF)

Above: B–17D in wartime camouflage, apparently OD overall. (USAF)

Below: An unusual scheme for an early Fortress, the white and OD of early USAAF coastal patrol squadrons. (USAF)

The CBI - Far East Area

On June 9th 1942 Flying Fortresses based in India fought through monsoons to knock out a Japanese base at Lashio in Burma. On July 21st a lone Fort was surrounded by 23 Japanese fighters while *en route* to bomb Rangoon. The crew fought them off, downing four in the process, and hit their target right on the button. The B-17 returned to base with two engines feathered and the rudder controls shot away, but still landed safely. These were typical missions flown by the B-17 crews in this theatre.

The European Theatre of Operations

To cover B-17 operations in this theatre in such a short text is impossible. Many fine books have been written which describe the campaign fully; the present writer will simply touch upon some of the most outstanding missions.

Assigned to the 8th Air Force were the 34th, 91st, 92nd, 94th, 95th, 96th, 97th, 100th, 301st, 303rd, 305th, 306th, 351st, 379th, 381st, 384th and the 385th Bomb Groups. These Groups produced eight Congressional Medals of Honour and 31 Distinguished Unit Citations while operating the B-17.

General Ira C. Eaker led a squadron of B-17's to bomb Rouen on August 17th 1942. This was the first daylight raid by the Americans on Hitler's " Fortress Europe ". Sgt. Kent L. West became the first American aerial gunner to shoot down a German fighter on this raid. All B-17's returned safely. While this was a very modest beginning it did prove one thing; the Yanks were there to do a job. Rougher times were ahead, but for the moment all had gone well. Next day they hit the marshalling yards at Amiens successfully. On the 21st things began to get rough as 20—25 German Fw 190's intercepted twelve Forts over the North Sea. The Forts claimed three Fw 190's shot down, and nine others as damaged or probables. All Forts made it back. On October 3rd the B-17's, which were making their thirteenth raid, hit St. Omer and Meaulre — and in turn were hit by a gaggle of German fighters estimated at close to 100. American gunners claimed 13 enemy fighters destroyed against no losses, but *Phyllis*, one of the Forts, came back with two engines out, half the controls shot away, landing gear mangled, a large hole in a wing and 200 holes in the fuselage. She had been the target of some 40 passes by German fighters, and had been worked over pretty well, but she still came home.

A little later a B 17 named (appropriately enough) *Flaming Jenny* came home from a raid with flames roaring through her from nose to tail, part of the left wing and left inboard engine gone and over 2,000 bullet holes in the skin. *Werewolf* limped home from a raid on Brest on one engine on January 23rd 1942. Such deeds were giving the Fortress a real reputation for " bringing 'em back alive ".

On August 17th 1943 the USAAF laid on a B-17 raid which almost ended the daylight attacks for good. The targets were Schweinfurt and Regensburg, the centres of production for ball bearings and aircraft respectively. Sixty Fortresses were shot down or lost on the mission, and many more were later written off due to battle damage sustained on these raids. Additional losses that week brought the total up to over 100 lost. The 8th simply could not stand another week of comparable losses if it were to survive. After a period of relatively light activity against carefully selected easy targets the 8th once more reached sufficient strength to hit Schweinfurt a knock-out blow, and on October 14th the B-17's took off and headed for the jinx target once again. This time another sixty bombers failed to return, and of those that did, over 200 had sustained battle damage, with many suffering crew casualties as well. The timely arrival at the front of the long-range P-51 escort fighter helped to keep losses within tolerable limits subsequently, and permitted continued daylight operations to keep up the pressure on the enemy.

The 100th Group lost so many aircraft during its early days that it became known as " The Bloody 100th ". Medals of Honour were won by crew men of the 92nd, 303rd (two), 305th (two), 306th and the 351st (two). Needless to say, the part played by the B-17 and its aircrews in the operations of the 8th was a major one.

The Mediterranean and Middle East

The 12th Air Force initially had the 2nd, the 68th, the 99th, and the 301st Bomb Groups assigned to it. The 5th Reconnaissance Group was also attached to the 12th, and part of its equipment consisted of B-17's. Eventually these Groups were transferred to the 15th Air Force as the 12th assumed a tactical rôle.

The first big B-17 raid took place on August 11th 1942 when they bombed two Axis ships in the harbour at Bengazi. On August 31st they hit Tobruk and Matruh. Small raids continued until November 18th, when the naval base at Bizerte was hit by a large force; this attack was followed by a full scale raid on the airfield at Tunis. January 12th 1943 found the B-17's hitting Castel Benito airfield in Tripoli, and on the 24th they all but wiped out the base at El Aouina. This is but a partial listing of the action on this front, and was culled from news headlines of the period.

The 5th Reconnaissance Group, while not primarily a B-17 unit, still flew a number of important missions with specially fitted Fortresses. These were mostly night photo-

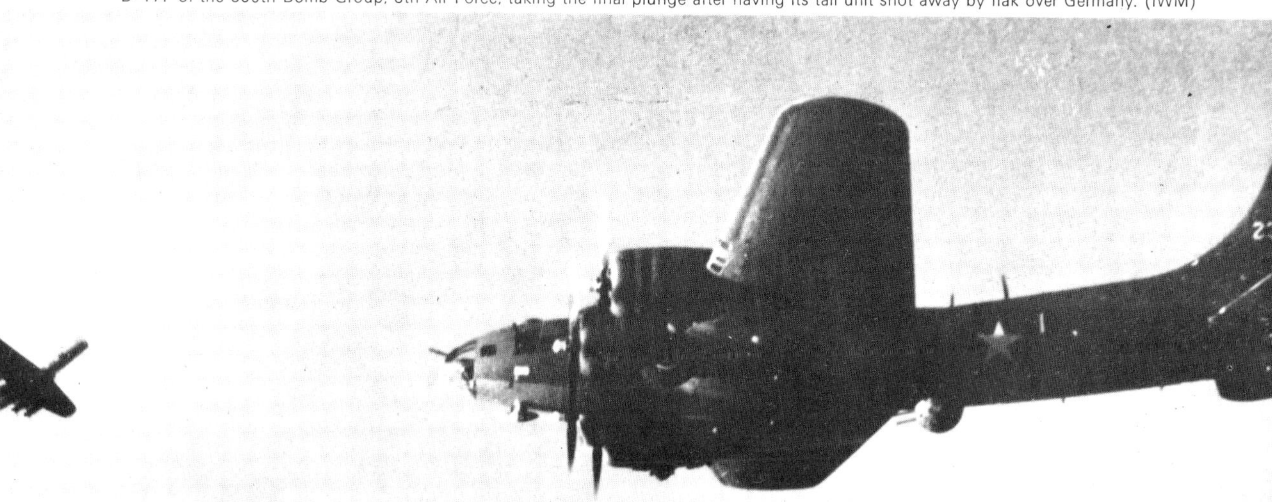

B–17F of the 305th Bomb Group, 8th Air Force, taking the final plunge after having its tail unit shot away by flak over Germany. (IWM)

A very interesting photograph showing a B–17D and two E's in formation probably late 1941 or early 1942. Note the D and one E have a four colour camouflage on the upper surfaces and all aircraft with the red and white rudder stripes. Rudder stripes and red centre to national insignia were used from Oct. 1941 to 15th May 1942.

graphic missions, as the B-17 could not only carry more cameras but also the large number of flares necessary to illuminate the target area to be photographed. The Fort was also better equipped to navigate after dark than a fighter-reconnaissance aircraft.

The Second Bombardment Group was one of the oldest bomber outfits in the Air Force, with a history dating back to World War I. It was also the oldest B-17 Group, as mentioned above. This unit operated B-17's throughout the entire war, from the very first day to the very last.

The Second may have been the only Group to win DUC's on successive days. On February 24th 1943 they fought their way through heavy opposition to the aircraft factories at Steyr — and did virtually the same next day when their target was the aircraft works at Regensburg, the target that had given the 8th so much trouble.

The 99th Group also won two DUC's. The first came for a raid on the airfield at Gerbini on July 5th 1943, and the second came on April 23rd 1944 when they bombed the aircraft factory at Wiener Neustadt against heavy enemy fighter opposition.

The 301st started its career with the 8th Air Force but after a few raids on targets in occupied France they were sent to North Africa. On April 6th 1943 they picked up a DUC when they flew through enemy shore-based flak as well as shipboard anti-aircraft fire to blast a convoy off Bizerte. They won another DUC as a member of the 15th Air Force on February 25th 1944, when they fought their way through heavy fighter opposition to bomb Regensburg, which was always heavily defended. The Group then took on a close support rôle and hit vital targets at Anzio and Cassino. They continued to support the ground forces during the invasion of Southern France and even flew missions in support of Russian troops advancing through the Balkans. They supported the Allied drive up the Po Valley.

Flying Fortresses operating out of Italy hit the same vital targets deep within Germany which the 8th was hitting from England. They also flew shuttle missions from Italy to Russia and back, bombing targets going and coming.

Foreign Service

The B-17 was flown in combat early in the war by the RAF when twelve B-17C's, known by the RAF as the Fortress I, began operational sorties with No. 90 Squadron on July 8th 1941. The USAAF had intended these aircraft to be used for training purposes only. Eight of these were lost, either in flying accidents or on operations, and the remaining Forts were withdrawn from combat operations. As more arrived they were sent to equip Nos. 206 and 220 Squadrons of RAF Coastal Command. The RAF received 45 B-17E's, which went to Coastal Command as the Fortress IIA. No. 59 Squadron was the first to be so equipped, and these aircraft quickly helped Costal Command to close the Atlantic Gap by virtue of their range.

Fortress III's equipped No. 214 Squadron, which was used on "cloak-and-dagger" operations along with No. 100 Group to jam enemy radar, and for other operations of this nature.

The Germans used a number of captured B-17's, which were known for security reasons as "Dornier Do 200's" and which were assigned to I/KG200. They fulfilled many rôles for the Axis; spy drops were frequently made from these aircraft. It has been said that others were painted in Allied markings and flew along with formations of bombers *en route* to a target; they would relay information as to speed, course, and altitude to the flak batteries along the bombers' route.

Post-War Service

After the war a number of B-17's were turned over to South American nations and served both as bombers and as cargo or passenger ships. A few are still flying today in various parts of South America as cargo haulers and as ASR machines. Others were sold to civilian companies after the war as surplus and converted to a number of peacetime uses including feeder airliners, aerial survey ships, forest fire fighters and company aircraft. In Sweden SAS flew a few of them as passenger aircraft; these were aircraft which had made forced landings in Sweden, and were turned over to the Swedish government. A small number of Fortresses were operated by the Israeli Air Force during their War of Independence in 1948, representing virtually their only bomber equipment at that time. The USAAF continued to operate a number in various rôles as drones, for weather reconnaissance and ASR purposes, and as test beds for various items.

Wartime Modifications

A number of modifications were tried at one time or another during the war. A B-17E was modified by Vega to take the Allison V-1710-89 engine as the XB-38, and these engines raised the maximum speed to 327 m.p.h. The prototype was subsequently destroyed by fire, and the project cancelled. Some war-weary B-17E's and F's were stripped of all but the bare minimum of equipment, packed with ten tons of Torpex, and operated as drones under the designation of BQ-7's. The plan was for a pilot to take off accompanied by a radio man who would then set the radio controls; the crewmen would bale out while the drone was taken over and guided to the target by a "mother" Fortress equipped for the job. After a couple crashed in England the project was abandoned. Other conversions included a V.I.P. transport designated the YC-108, a tanker version under the designation XC-108B and a number of long range reconnaissance versions designated the F-9, F-9A and F-9B depending on the camera array carried.

The XB-40 was perhaps the worst flop experienced by Boeing in its conversions. A "gun ship" designed to provide protection for formations, it could not even keep up with them. The B-17H was an air-sea rescue version equipped to drop a fully equipped boat to crews downed at sea. After the war ended many equipped as drones under the designation of either DB-17's or QB-17's, and were used as targets for various missiles. Whatever the job it was called upon to perform, the B-17 did it — and usually did it remarkably well.

Above: B-17C of the 11th Bomb Group,
probably the Squadron Leader's aircraft. (USAF)

Above: B-17D, 7th Bomb Group,
note US ARMY under the wings. (USAF)

Above: Nice flying shot of a B-17D, note the Wright Field insignia on aft fuselage. (USAF)

Below: Early B-17E showing off its new lines flying past Boeing's private mountain. (Boeing)

Above: B–17F at White Horse, Yukon, en-route to the 11th Air Force in the Aleutians probably destined for the 36th Bomb Squadron. Note early type ASV radar under wings for anti-shipping work. (Ken Howat via Ted Hooton)

Above: B–17E of the 7th Bomb Group, Pacific Theatre of Operations, serial 19122, revving up on the newly laid runway at Guadalcanal, Dec. 1942.   (USMC)

Above: B–17E of the 5th Bomb Group, 13th Air Force, SWPA, on Sea Search duties over the Pacific. The photo of the aircraft has quite obviously been superimposed over the background. (USAF)

Below: A 12th Air Force B–17F taking off from Oujda landing-ground, Morocco, June 1943. Note yellow surround to national insignia. (USAF)

Above: 'Peggy D', a B–17E of the 97th Bomb Group, the first operational B–17 Group of the 8th Air Force, ETO. This particular aircraft took part in the first mission, a raid on a railway marshalling yard at Rouen on the 17th August 1942. Note two tone green upper surface camouflage. (IWM)

Above and below: B–17E's of the 97th Bomb Group, 8th Air Force, ETO. (IWM)

Above and below: 'Delta Rebel 2' a B–17F of the 91st Bomb Group, 322nd Bomb Squadron, 8th Air Force. 14 swastika's and 26 bombs. Note the whip aerials under the nose and above the aft canopy, medium green splotches on fin and rudder. Serial believed to be 25057, aircraft letter T. (USAF)

Above: 'Memphis Belle' on its return to the US after completing 25 combat missions with the 91st BG, 324th BS, 8th AF. B–17F, serial 124485, code DF–A. (USAF)

Above: B–17F, 91st BG, 323rd BS, 8th AF, taking off from Bassingbourn, Cambs., on its first mission using the new external bomb racks. 16th Sept. 1943. Yellow surround to national insignia, star and bar in grey all positions. (USAF)

Above and below: 'Sad Sack', 91st BG, 324th BS, 8th AF, winging its way over the English countryside on a practice mission, 10th July 1944. Lower photo shows 'Sad Sack' on day of retirement from 91st BG. (USAF)

Above: 'Idiot's Delight' after completing 50 successful missions without one abortion taxying into dispersal area upon its return from Berlin on 22nd March 1944. 91st BG 8th AF. (USAF)

Above: 'Lady Luck' a B–17F of the 91st BG, 324th BS, 8th AF, on its dispersal area at Bassingbourn Cambs., U.K., home base of the Group. (USAF)

Above: 'The Careful Virgin' with 11 swastikas and 50 bombs to its credit, a B–17F of the 91st BG, 322nd BS, 8th AF. (USAF)

Below: The personal B–17F of Brig. General Robert B. Williams parked on the taxi strip at Bassingbourn during a visit to the 91st Bomb Group. (USAF)

Above: 'Rebel's Revenge' flying over the English countryside on a practice mission, 25th Sept. 1943. Yellow surround to national insignia. (USAF)

Below: 91st Bomb Group laying their eggs on a German target, some dropping 9, some 11 and some 12. (IWM)

Above: A mixed formation of Fortresses of the 91st BG, 401st BS, 8th AF, heading out for a German target. (USAF)

Below: B–17F, 96th BG, on its dispersal area, P–51B's of the 364th FG, overhead. (James C. Field)

Below: B–17G's of the 96th BG, 338th BS. Note codes fore and aft of national insignia. (James C. Field)

Above: B–17G of the 96th BG, 337th BS, 8th AF. (James C. Field)

Below: Fine flying shot of vic of B–17G's of 96th BG, 413rd BS, 8th AF. Note unusual position of J in code, QJ–K equipped with Cheyenne tail turret. (James C. Field)

Excellent flying shot of B–17F 'Kipling's Error III' of the 96th Bomb Group, 8th Air Force. (James C. Field)

With contrails streaming four B–17G's of the 96th Bomb Group, 337th Bomb Squadron, 8th Air Force head out for a German target. (James C. Field)

Nice flying shot showing upper surface details of B–17G's of the 92nd Bomb Group, 325th Bomb Squadron, 8th Air Force, high over occupied France. (James C. Field)

Two fine shots of Fortresses over Europe on their way to the targets, upper photograph shows a formation of the 303rd Bomb Group, lower photograph, group unknown. (USAF)

Above: 'Hell's Angels', missions completed, points her nose for the Atlantic on the start of her return to the US. B–17F, 303rd BG, 358th BS, Code VK–D, serial 124577. (USAF)

Left: RQ–R a B–17G of the 351st BG 409th BS 8th AF, which forced landed at Bultofto, Sweden, on 21st June 1944 and was interned. (via E. A. Munday)

Above and below: Formating aircraft of the 379th Bomb Group, see colour illustration. (USAF)

Below: 'Busy Baby' a B–17G of the 379th Bomb Group, 524th Bomb Squadron, photograph taken 8th April 1944. (USAF)

Above and below: Nice flying shots of a B–17G of the 379th Bomb Group, 524th Bomb Squadron, 8th AF. (MOD)

Above: Formation of B–17G's, 381st BG, 533rd BS, 8th AF. VP–X has blue surround to fuselage insignia red surround to wing insignia. (USAF)

Below: 'Happy Bottom' an immaculate B–17G of the 381st BG, 532nd BS, 8th AF. (USAF)

Above: 'Winsome Winn'—'Hilda' of the 381st BG. 534th BS. 8th AF. Note red surround to national insignia (USAF)

Above: A B–17F of the 381st BG, 532nd BS, 8th AF, heading out for a target in Europe. (USAF)

Above: 'Little America' UK bound on return trip from target in Europe, B–17F, 384th BG, 544th BS, 8th AF. Code BK–S, see colour illustration (USAF)

Below: B–17G of the 398th Bomb Group, 603rd Bomb Squadron, 8th Air Force, forced landed on the beach at Sandwich Bay, Kent, just a few miles short of the emergency airfield at Manston, damaged by flak over Europe. All red fin, note OD anti-glare panel above tail turret, code 30–A. (Ray E. Bowers)

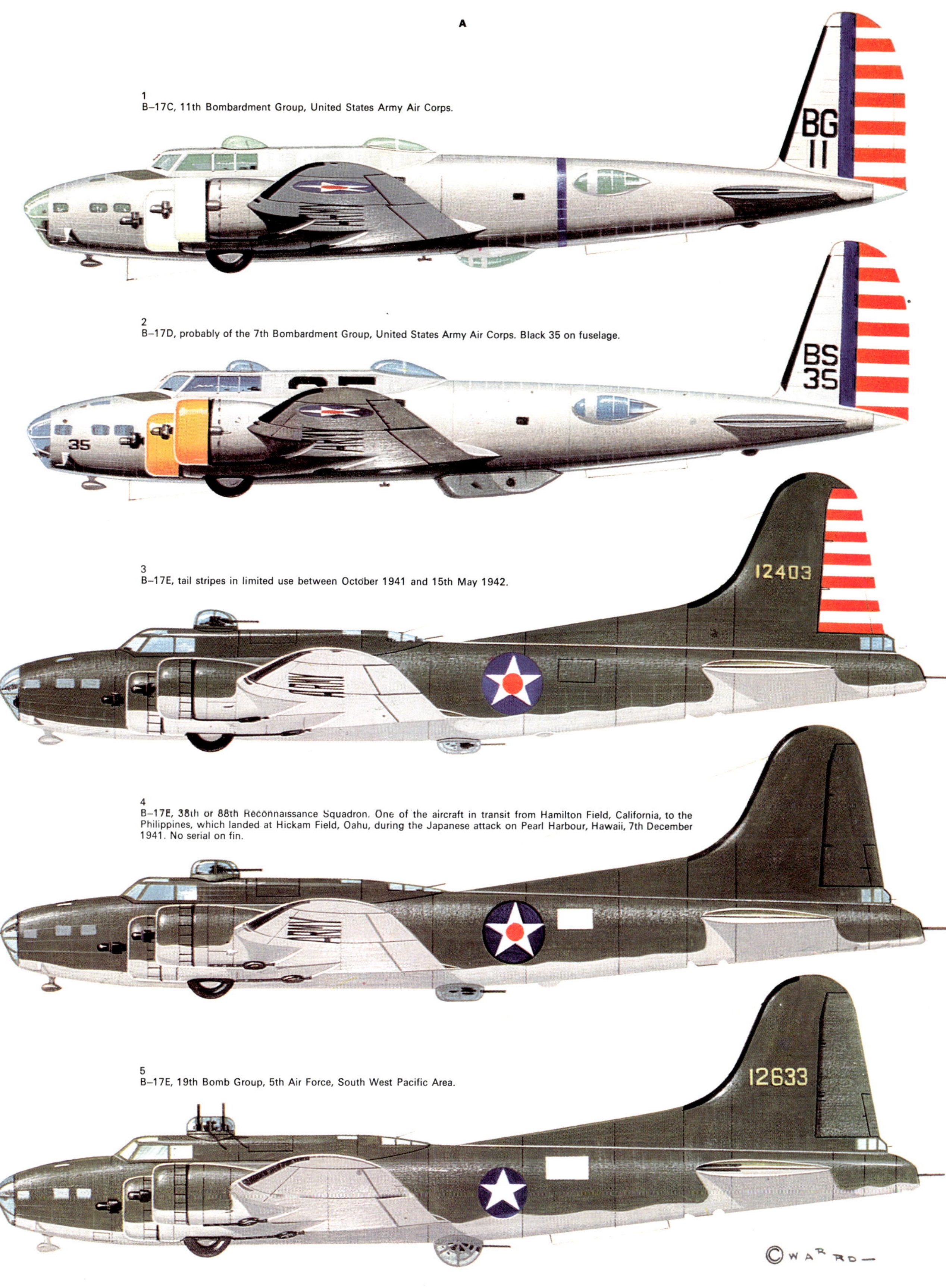

1
B–17C, 11th Bombardment Group, United States Army Air Corps.

2
B–17D, probably of the 7th Bombardment Group, United States Army Air Corps. Black 35 on fuselage.

3
B–17E, tail stripes in limited use between October 1941 and 15th May 1942.

4
B–17E, 38th or 88th Reconnaissance Squadron. One of the aircraft in transit from Hamilton Field, California, to the Philippines, which landed at Hickam Field, Oahu, during the Japanese attack on Pearl Harbour, Hawaii, 7th December 1941. No serial on fin.

5
B–17E, 19th Bomb Group, 5th Air Force, South West Pacific Area.

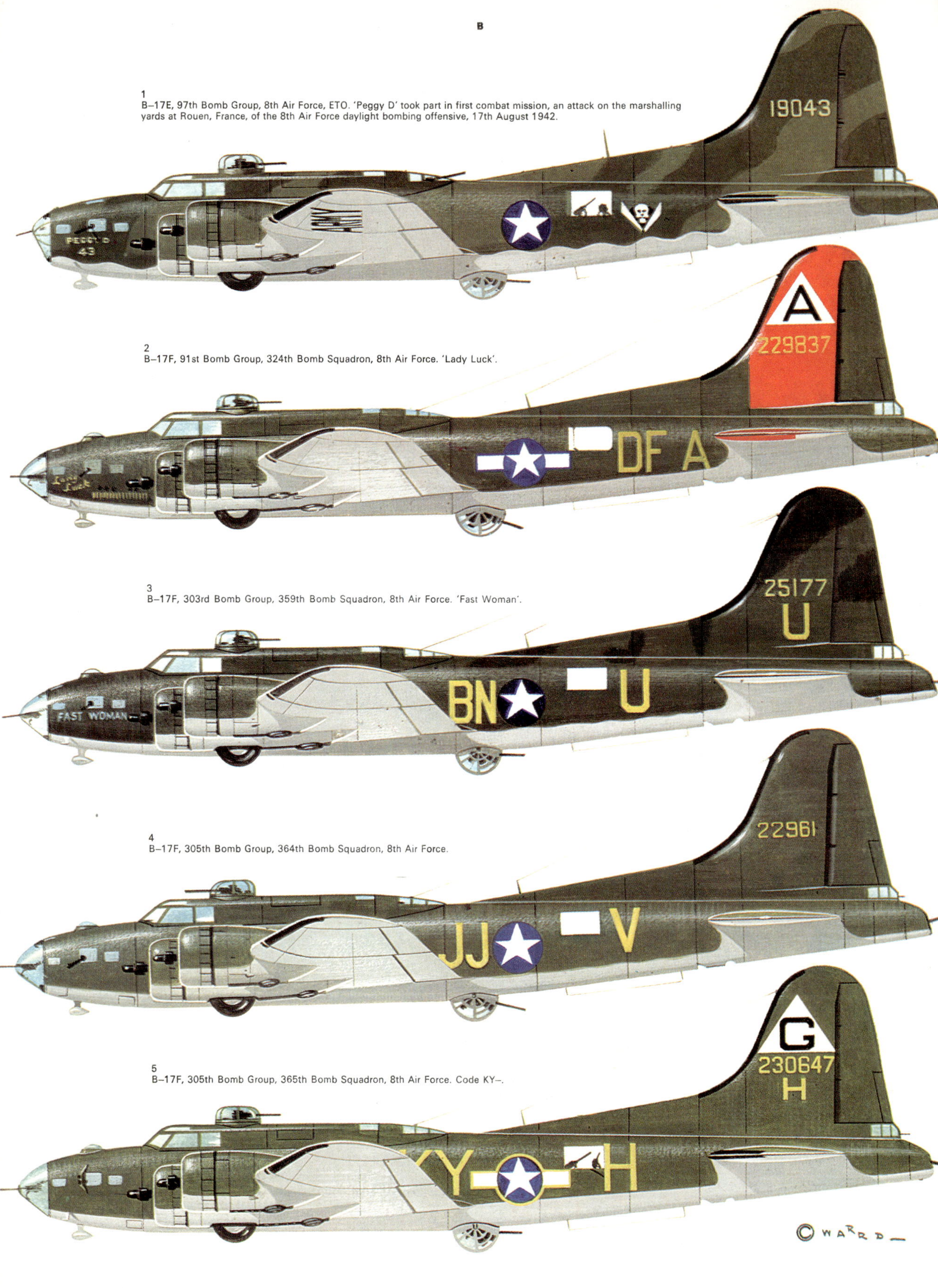

1
B–17E, 97th Bomb Group, 8th Air Force, ETO. 'Peggy D' took part in first combat mission, an attack on the marshalling yards at Rouen, France, of the 8th Air Force daylight bombing offensive, 17th August 1942.

2
B–17F, 91st Bomb Group, 324th Bomb Squadron, 8th Air Force. 'Lady Luck'.

3
B–17F, 303rd Bomb Group, 359th Bomb Squadron, 8th Air Force. 'Fast Woman'.

4
B–17F, 305th Bomb Group, 364th Bomb Squadron, 8th Air Force.

5
B–17F, 305th Bomb Group, 365th Bomb Squadron, 8th Air Force. Code KY–.

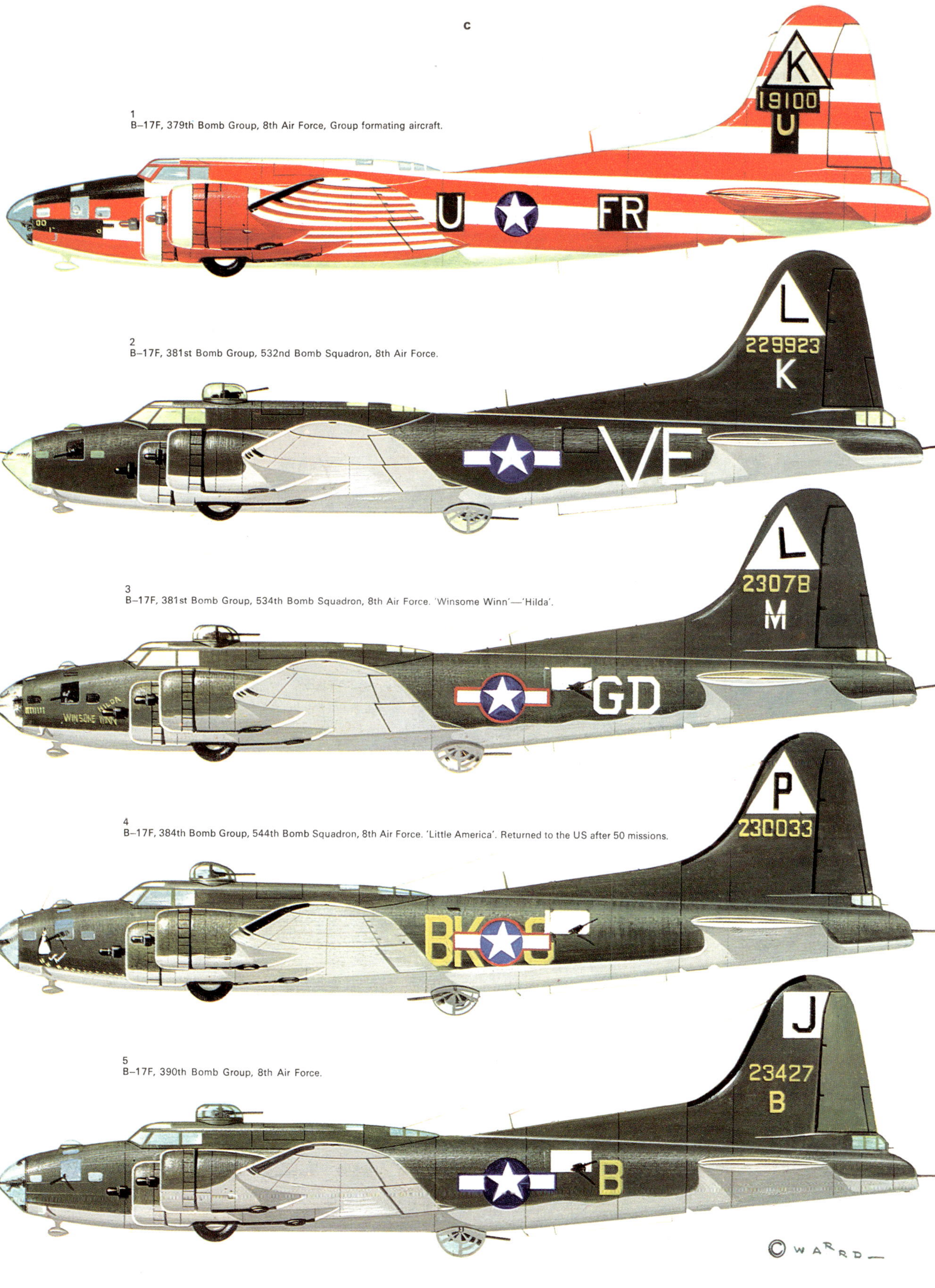

c

1
B–17F, 379th Bomb Group, 8th Air Force, Group formating aircraft.

2
B–17F, 381st Bomb Group, 532nd Bomb Squadron, 8th Air Force.

3
B–17F, 381st Bomb Group, 534th Bomb Squadron, 8th Air Force. 'Winsome Winn'—'Hilda'.

4
B–17F, 384th Bomb Group, 544th Bomb Squadron, 8th Air Force. 'Little America'. Returned to the US after 50 missions.

5
B–17F, 390th Bomb Group, 8th Air Force.

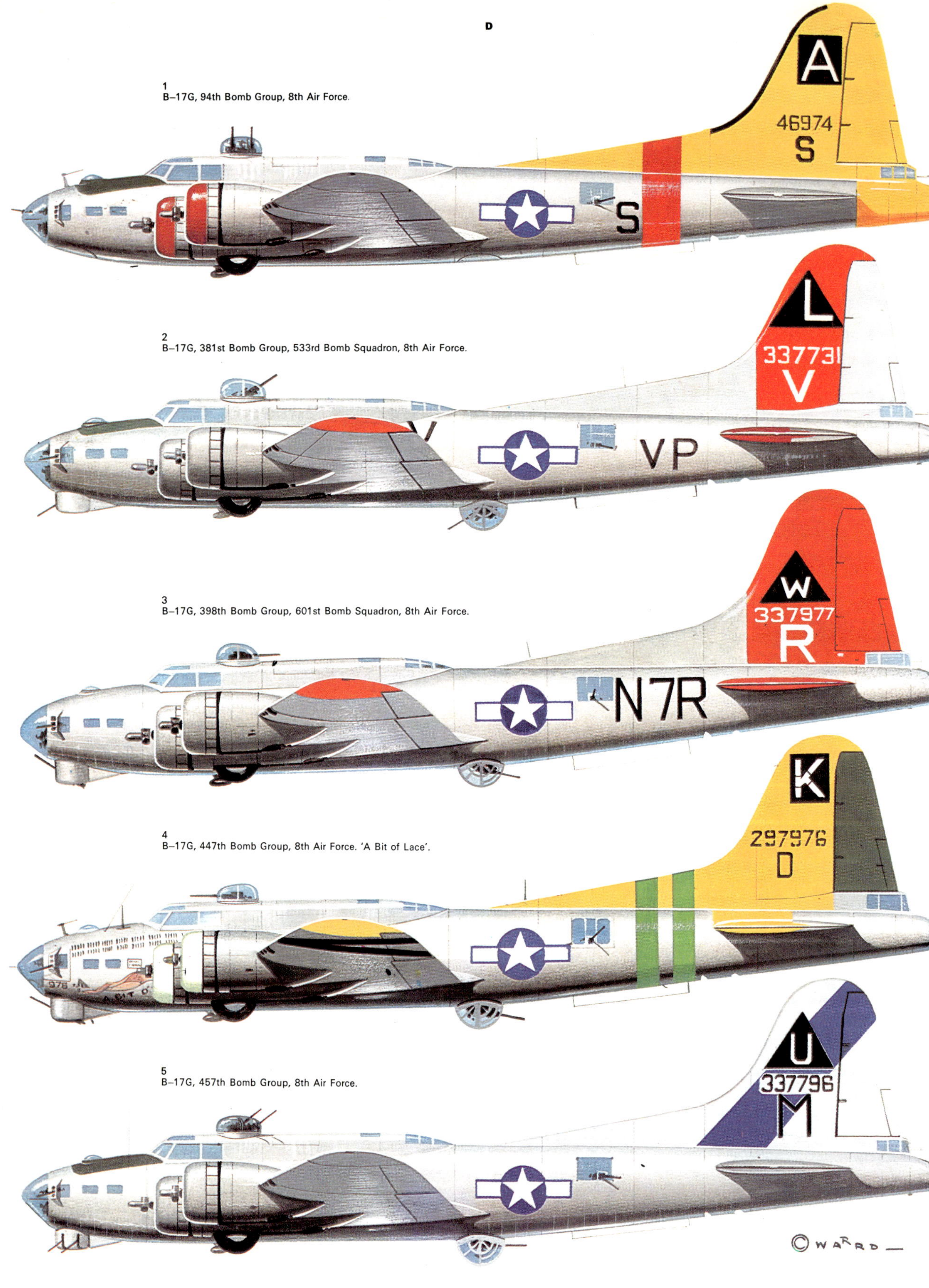

D
1
B-17G, 94th Bomb Group, 8th Air Force.
46974
S
A
S
2
B-17G, 381st Bomb Group, 533rd Bomb Squadron, 8th Air Force.
337731
L
V
VP
3
B-17G, 398th Bomb Group, 601st Bomb Squadron, 8th Air Force.
337977
W
R
N7R
4
B-17G, 447th Bomb Group, 8th Air Force. 'A Bit of Lace'.
297976
K
D
5
B-17G, 457th Bomb Group, 8th Air Force.
337796
U
M
WARD

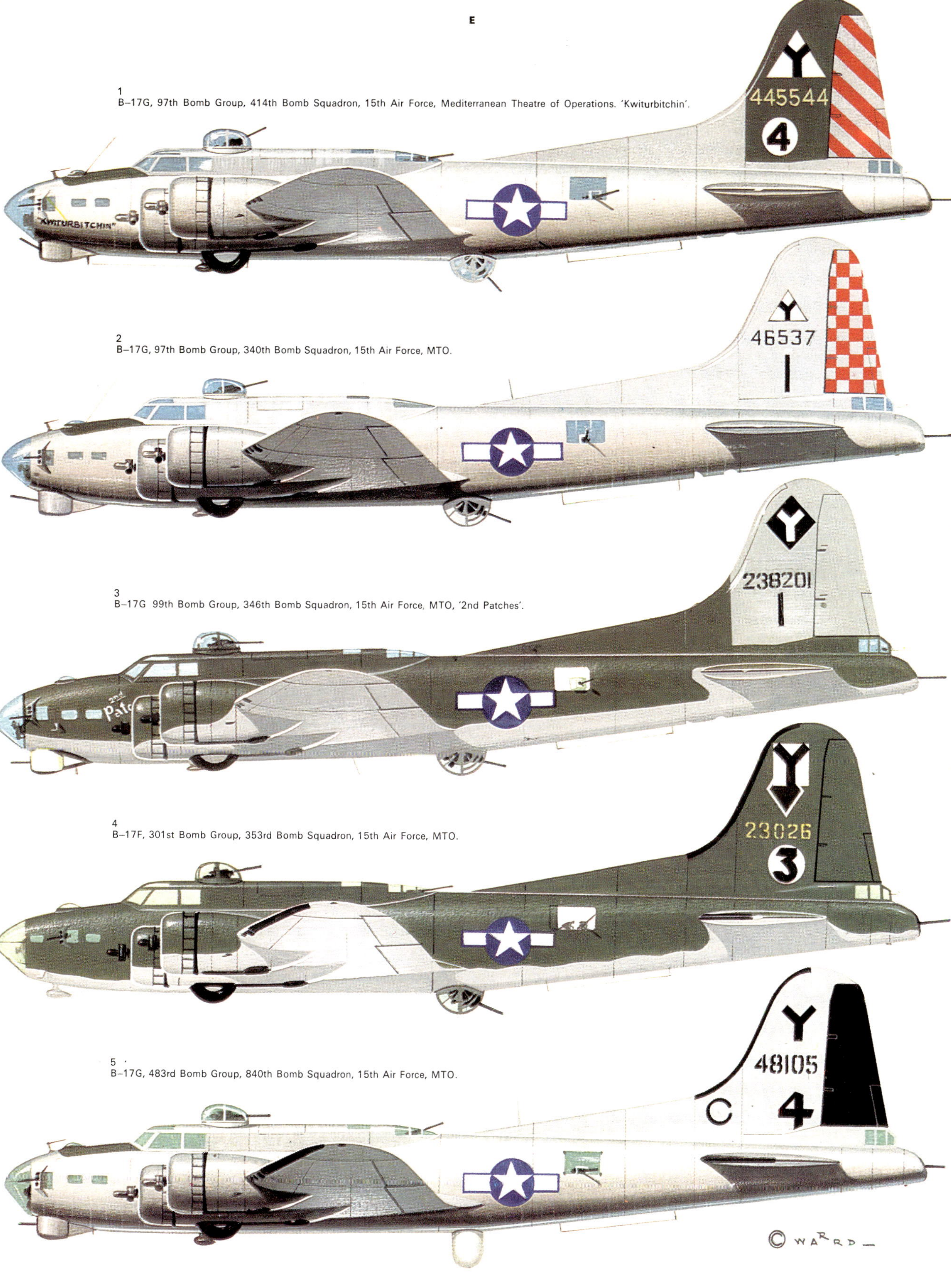

1
B–17G, 97th Bomb Group, 414th Bomb Squadron, 15th Air Force, Mediterranean Theatre of Operations. 'Kwiturbitchin'.

2
B–17G, 97th Bomb Group, 340th Bomb Squadron, 15th Air Force, MTO.

3
B–17G 99th Bomb Group, 346th Bomb Squadron, 15th Air Force, MTO, '2nd Patches'.

4
B–17F, 301st Bomb Group, 353rd Bomb Squadron, 15th Air Force, MTO.

5
B–17G, 483rd Bomb Group, 840th Bomb Squadron, 15th Air Force, MTO.

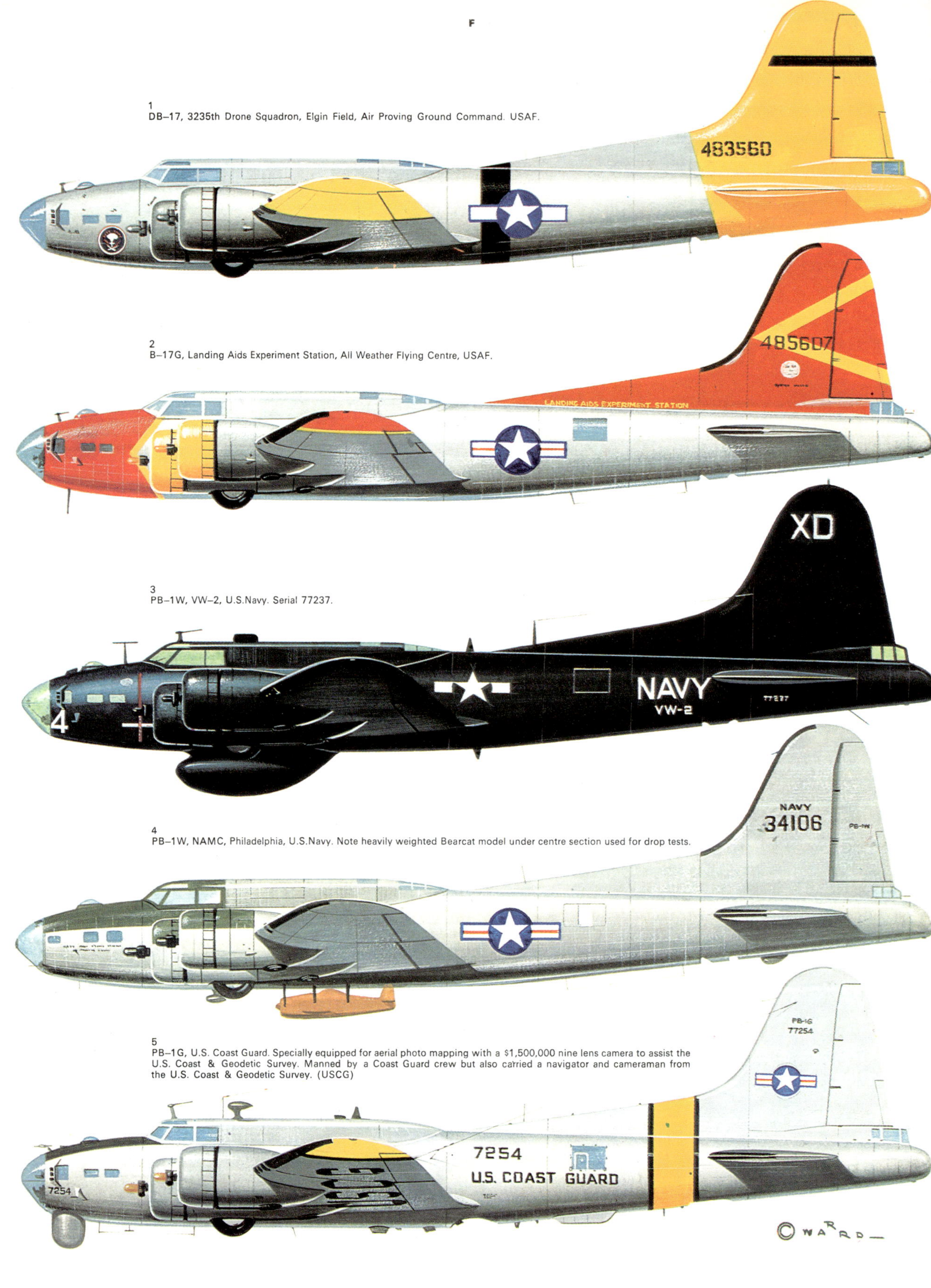

1
DB–17, 3235th Drone Squadron, Elgin Field, Air Proving Ground Command. USAF.

2
B–17G, Landing Aids Experiment Station, All Weather Flying Centre, USAF.

3
PB–1W, VW–2, U.S.Navy. Serial 77237.

4
PB–1W, NAMC, Philadelphia, U.S.Navy. Note heavily weighted Bearcat model under centre section used for drop tests.

5
PB–1G, U.S. Coast Guard. Specially equipped for aerial photo mapping with a $1,500,000 nine lens camera to assist the U.S. Coast & Geodetic Survey. Manned by a Coast Guard crew but also carried a navigator and cameraman from the U.S. Coast & Geodetic Survey. (USCG)

1
Fortress I, No. 90 Squadron, Royal Air Force. Used as a high-altitude day bomber. Code WP+F

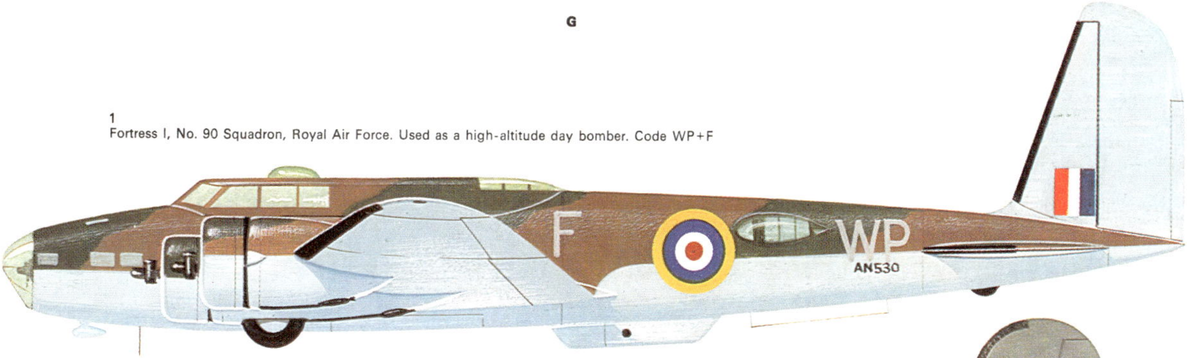

2
Fortress II or probably more correctly B–17E. Something of a mystery ship as no official records exist of this aircraft in RAF service. Crashed on mountainside north of Blackcat Gap, Wau, New Guinea, where the remains still exist. RAAF?

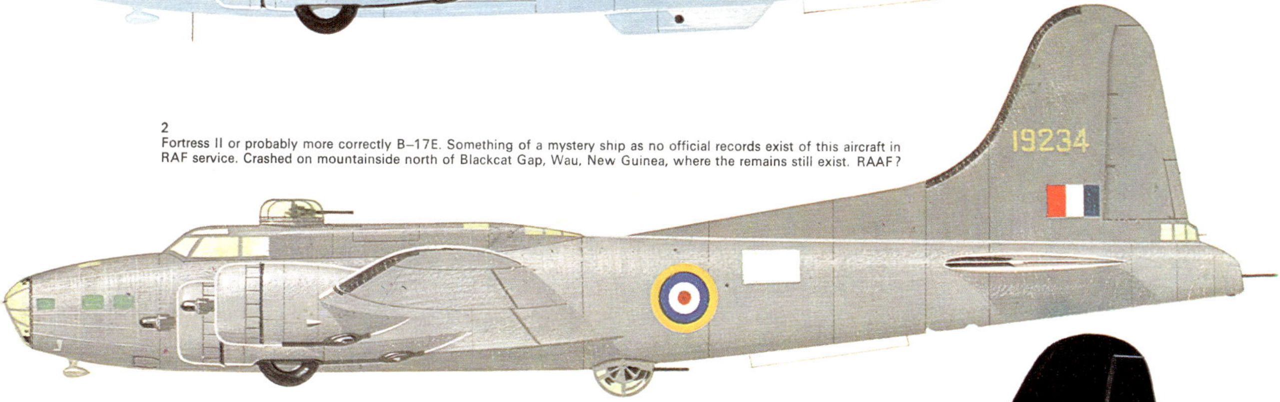

3
Fortress III, No. 214 'Federated Malay States' Squadron, No. 100 Bomber Support Group, Royal Air Force. Employed on radio counter-measure duties, the detection and jamming of enemy radio and radar equipment. Code BU–H, Serial KJ101.

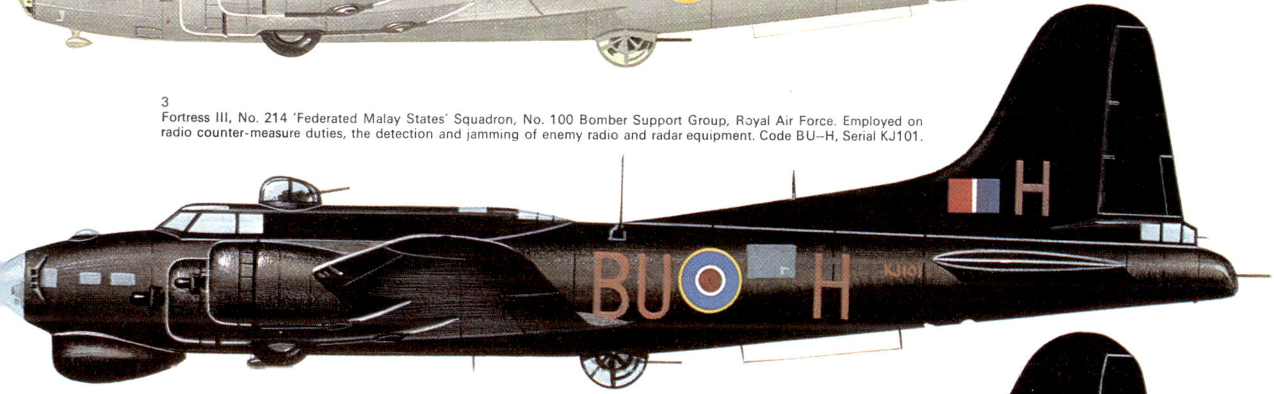

4
Fortress III, No. 223 Squadron, No. 100 Bomber Support Group, Royal Air Force. Duties as above, Code 6G–F, Serial KJ109.

5
Fortress GRIIA, No. 251 Squadron, Coastal Command, Royal Air Force. Employed on Meteorological Reconnaissance and Air Sea Rescue duties. Serial FK197.

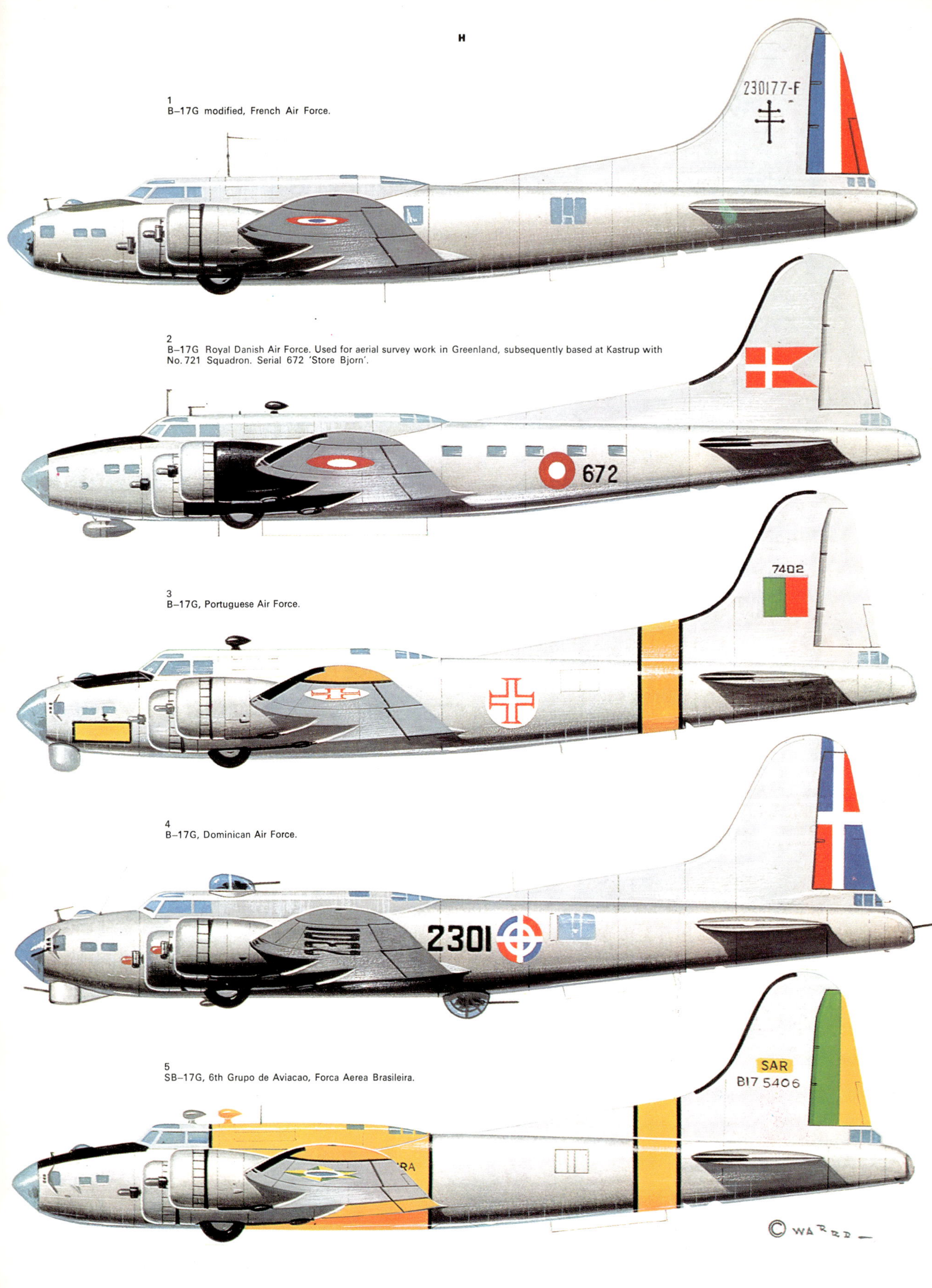

1
B–17G modified, French Air Force.

2
B–17G Royal Danish Air Force. Used for aerial survey work in Greenland, subsequently based at Kastrup with No. 721 Squadron. Serial 672 'Store Bjorn'.

3
B–17G, Portuguese Air Force.

4
B–17G, Dominican Air Force.

5
SB–17G, 6th Grupo de Aviacao, Forca Aerea Brasileira.

Above: Fortresses of the 390th Bomb Group, 8th Air Force, taking off for a mission over Europe, late 1943 or early 1944. (via E. A. Munday)

Right: B–17G of the 401st BG dropping its bombs on a German target. Note yellow diagonal tail stripe outlined black, group identification S on black diamond. (via E. A. Munday)

Above: After forced landing in a small English field this B–17G of the 401st BG was flown out with the assistance of 12 rockets attached to the under surface of the wings. The successful take-off and return flight to base was made by Capt. Richard C. Bolub. (USAF)

Below: 'Sharkmouthed' B–17G 'Sandusky-JoAnn' of the 447th Bomb Group, 8th Air Force. (Charles E. Brown)

Fine flying shot of 'A Bit of Lace', B–17G, 447th Bomb Group, below practice formations by the 447th BG. (Photos Charles E. Brown)

Above: B-17G of the 452nd Bomb Group, 8th Air Force, note late type beam gun position.

Right: OD camouflaged B-17G of the 452nd Bomb Group, the shot clearly shows the upper surface group marking.

Above: 457th Bomb Group B-17G with diagonal blue tail stripe, serial 337796. (Fred C. Dickey, Jr.)

Above: A B-17G of the 487th BG taxying out from its dispersal area after repairs at Manston. (Ray E. Bowers)

Below: A B-17G of the 34th Bomb Group, the last group in the 8th Air Force to be equipped with the type. Note red fin, tailplane and wing stripes. (via E. A. Munday)

Top: B–17G, 2nd Bomb Group, 15th Air Force, MTO. Serial 46440, the last three numerals repeated on nose. Vapour trails from a pair of P–38's in the background. (USAF)

Above: Formation of B–17G's of the 2nd Bomb Group, 15th AF, over Bleckhammer, Germany, 7th July 1944. Aircraft belong, to the 20th Bomb Squadron. (USAF)

Left: B–17G's of the 97th Bomb Group, note tail marking variations.
(via E. A. Munday)

Below: Fortresses of the 97th BG, 414th BS, with vapour trails streaming leave a target in Northern Italy. Diagonal red on bare metal rudder stripes. (USAF)

Above: A pair of 99th Bomb Group B–17G's banking low over the Alps, late 1944. (USAF)

Above: 'Yankee Doodle' a B–17F of the 99th Bomb Group, probably the 347th Bomb Squadron on its way to bomb a ball-bearing plant in Turin, Italy, on 5th November 1943. Note early group marking. (USAF)

Right and below: '2nd Patches' a B–17G of the 99th Bomb Group, 15th Air Force, MTO. Probably of the 346th Bomb Squadron, in the past this aircraft has been reputed to carry a 'sharkmouth' on the chin turret, the bottom photograph proves this not to have been the case. See colour illustration. (Right via F. F. Smith, bottom USAF)

Fine shot of B–17G's of the 97th Bomb Group with P–38 escorts heading for the marshalling yards at Linz, Austria. 340th Bomb Squadron. (USAF)

Fortresses of the 97th Bomb Group, 15th Air Force, MTO, flying through heavy flak after bombing the Schwechat Oil Refinery at Vienna, Austria, on 10th September 1944. (USAF)

Above: 301st Bomb Group, 353rd Bomb Squadron Fortresses high over the Alps. Note the group marking painted over an older diamond marking. 3 on white disc indicates 353rd BS. (IWM)

Above: Nice flying shot of radar equipped B–17G of the 483rd Bomb Group, 840th Bomb Squadron, 15th Air Force. See colour illustration. (USAF)

Above: B–17F showing one of the very early Group identification markings, a hollow triangle which appears to have been superimposed over the black circle marking of another Group. (IWM)

Below: Enlargement of photo taken from Luftwaffe POW shot down in Africa shows a captured B–17G in Luftwaffe markings. (USAF)

Above: B–17H Dumbo, 6th Emergency Rescue Squadron based on Okinawa 1946. 'Pacific Tramp'. (Boeing)

Above: DB–17 Flying Fortress 'Director', used by the 3235th Drone Squadron to control QB–17 'Drones'. The 'Director' shown above took off from Elgin Field, Florida, headquarters of the Air Proving Ground Command, with a drone which it flew to Washington DC on 13th January 1947. The 'beeper' pilot flew the drone from the 'Director' for the entire flight. (USAF)

Below: Line-up of DB–17 and QB–17's at Elgin Field. See colour illustration. (USAF)

Below: B–17G of Air Proving Ground Command, note U.S. Air Force on nose. (R. W. Harrison-L. Paul)

Above: PB–1W, Serial 77237, U.S. Navy, in overall midnite blue scheme, note radome. (Peter M. Bowers)

Above: PB–1G of the United States Coast Guard, with moulded plywood lifeboat. (USCG)

Above: Nose detail B–17F. (USAF)

Above: Nose detail B–17G. (USAF)

Above: PB–1G, USCG. (via R. C. B. Ashworth)

Below: This PB–1G served for 12 years as a special aerial photo mapping aircraft with the U.S. Coast & Geodetic Survey, armed with a $1,500,000 nine lens mapping camera. The PB–1G was a modified B–17H. (USCG)

Above: Fortress I, AN521, No. 90 Squadron, RAF. Used on high-altitude day bombing raids over Europe for which role it proved to be quite useless. (IWM)

Above: Fortress GR.I, No. 206 Squadron, Coastal Command, RAF. (IWM)

Above: Fortress GR.IIA, No. 251 Squadron formating with a Hudson GR.V, used on meteorological reconnaissance and air-sea rescue duties. (R. C. B. Ashworth)

Above and below: Fortress GR.IIA's of No. 220 Squadron, note ASV radar on J. (Photos IWM)

Above: Fortress GR.IIA of No. 220 Squadron taking off from Lagens airfield, Azores. (IWM)

Left and below: A pair of GR.IIA's of No. 220 Squadron low down over the drink, the lower photograph also shows the upper aircraft, V FK212. The nose and under wing radar aerials have on both photographs been retouched out due to wartime security precautions. (Photos IWM)

Above: B–17G of the French Air Force, see colour illustration. (R. C. B. Ashworth)

Above and below: Civilianised B–17G's used by the French Institute Geographique Nationale. F–BGSP was 44–8846 ex-305th Bomb Group, USAAF. (Photos R. C. B. Ashworth)

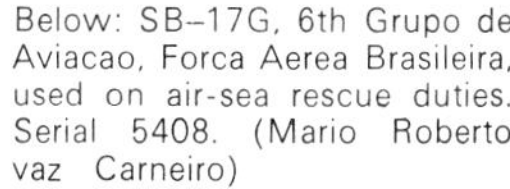

Right: SB–17G of the Brazilian Air Force, note modified chin position, used on air-sea rescue duties. (Mario Roberto vaz Carneiro)

Below: SB–17G, 6th Grupo de Aviacao, Forca Aerea Brasileira, used on air-sea rescue duties. Serial 5408. (Mario Roberto vaz Carneiro)

Above: B–17G modified for air-sea rescue duties. Portuguese Air Force, see colour illustration. (S. P. Peltz)

Above and below: B–17G modified for transport duties by the Royal Danish Air Force. Both photographs show same aircraft 672. (Jacob Stoppel)

Below: B–17G in close formation with a pair of Spitfire IX's, Israeli Defence Force/Air Force. (S. P. Peltz)

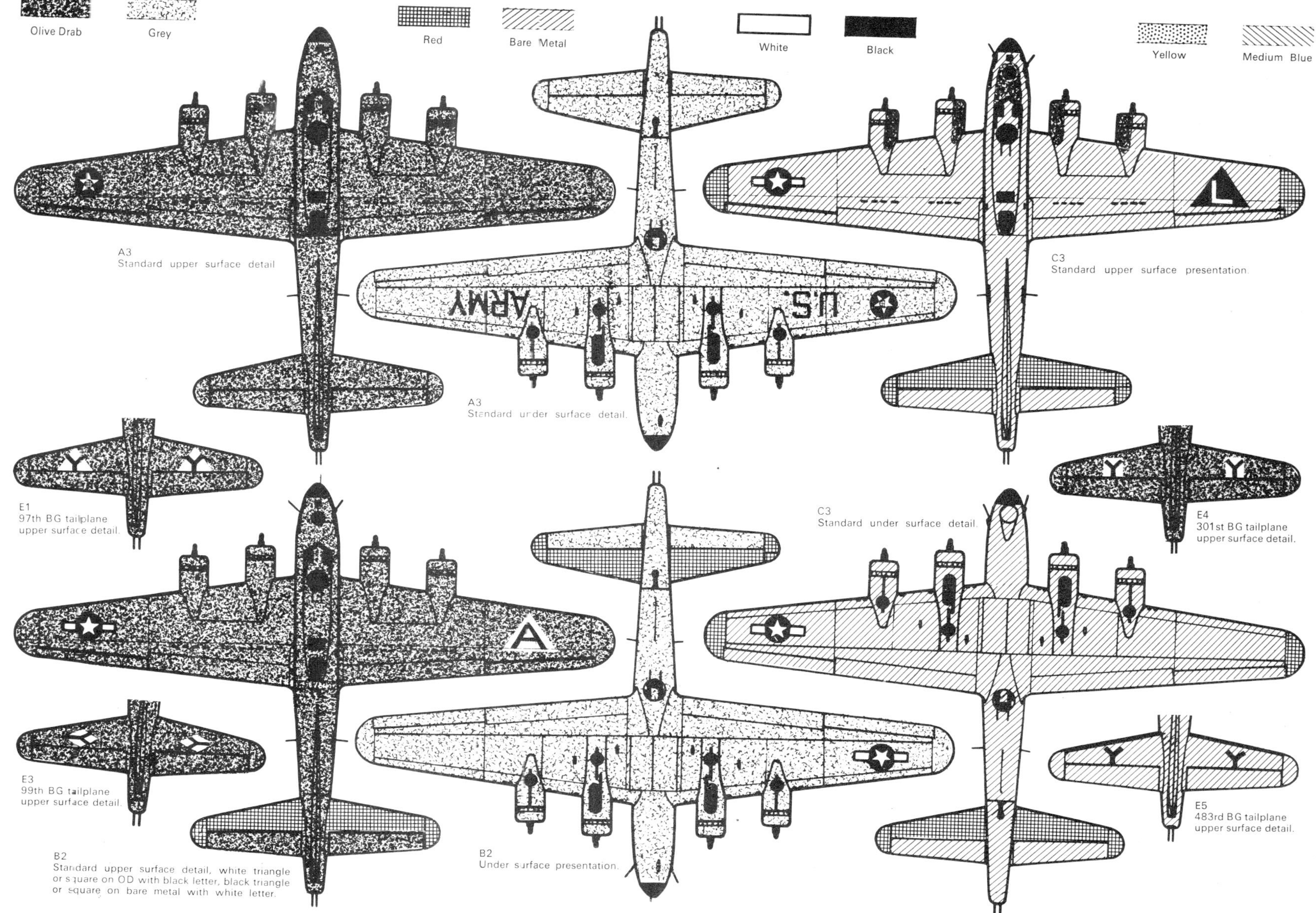

Olive Drab
Grey
Red
Bare Metal
White
Black
Yellow
Medium Blue

A3
Standard upper surface detail.

C3
Standard upper surface presentation.

ARMY U.S.

A3
Standard under surface detail.

C3
Standard under surface detail.

E1
97th BG tailplane upper surface detail.

E4
301st BG tailplane upper surface detail.

E3
99th BG tailplane upper surface detail.

E5
483rd BG tailplane upper surface detail.

B2
Standard upper surface detail, white triangle or square on OD with black letter, black triangle or square on bare metal with white letter.

B2
Under surface presentation.

C1
Upper surface detail.
G1
Upper surface camouflage pattern.
G1
Under surface detail, overall Sky Blue.
C1
Under surface detail.
Sky Blue
Dark Earth
Dark Green
D4
Upper surface detail. Originally this aircraft had a yellow rudder serial on bare metal panel within yellow surround and Group letter K without stencil breaks. The yellow rudder was damaged by flak and replaced with an OD one, at a later date the fin was re-painted yellow with the serial applied direct on the yellow, the black square and K were also repainted in a slightly different position; at this time the K was stencilled on as per the colour illustration.
D4
Under surface detail.
F1
Upper and under surfaces identical.
G3/4
Upper surface detail, under surface overall black, no national insignia.
Bright Green